PENGUIN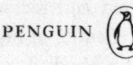

PENGUIN ENG
GENERAL EDITOR: CE

SELECTED POEMS OF
THOMAS GRAY, CHARLES CHURCHILL
AND WILLIAM COWPER

THOMAS GRAY was born in 1716, the son of a London scrivener, and was educated at Eton and Peterhouse, Cambridge. In 1741, the year after his father's death, he moved to Cambridge and lived there for the rest of his life. Gray was one of the forerunners of the Romantic movement in England, and his works, mostly lyrics and Pindaric odes, display an interest in the self, in society and in literary history, all of which were to become hallmarks of Romanticism. His most famous work is the *Elegy Written in a Country Churchyard*. He was also a well-known letter-writer, notably to Horace Walpole, with whom he had attended Eton and who published some of his work. His last major poems were published by Walpole in 1757, and his later years were largely devoted to antiquarian studies and travel around the British Isles. During this period he wrote, amongst other things, poetry that imitated early Norse and Welsh verse, an area of literature in which he took considerable interest, and a journal of a visit to the Lakes. He died in Cambridge in 1771.

CHARLES CHURCHILL was born in 1731, the son of a poor clergyman. Educated at Westminster (with William Cowper) and (fleetingly) St John's College, Cambridge, he was ordained in 1756, probably out of economic necessity. He succeeded his father as curate of St John's, Westminster, and lived in poverty until 1761, when the publication of *The Rosciad* and *The Apology* brought him money and recognition. His existence became more and more worldly, and he continued to write satirical verse, notably for the *North Briton*, a radical opposition journal authored by his friend John Wilkes, a notorious political activist and debauché. The targets of his satirical poetry were varied and included the Scots and Scotland, politicians of the day, enemies of his friend Wilkes, Dr Johnson and the acting profession. He died in 1764 whilst on his way to visit Wilkes in France, aged only thirty-three.

WILLIAM COWPER was born in 1731; the eldest son of a Hertford-shire rector, his mother died when he was six. He was educated at a private school (where he was bullied), and at Westminster, where Charles Churchill was a contemporary. Religion and unhappiness dominated his life. Called to the Bar in 1754, he soon suffered the first of several mental and emotional breakdowns. From here onward he suffered from acute melancholia and turned to evangeli-cal Christianity. In 1765 he went to live in Huntingdon with the Reverend Morley Unwin and his wife Mary, and on the death of the clergyman Cowper moved with Mrs Unwin to Olney. Here he met John Newton, the evangelical curate with whom he co-wrote *Olney Hymns* (1779). Cowper's mental health was always variable (he made one of a number of suicide attempts during this period) and, despite periodic recoveries, the death in 1796 of Mrs Unwin prompted the onset of a severe depression which blighted the last four years of his life. He began writing late in life, in a style that presaged full-blown Romanticism, producing hymns, religious poetry, lyrical works and his gentle mock-epic *The Task* (1785). He left behind many letters and autobiographical writings, and in 1816 the moving autobiographical *Memoir* was published. He died in 1800, not long after writing the desolate poem 'The Castaway'.

KATHERINE TURNER has held lectureships at Oriel, Balliol and St Hugh's College, Oxford, and is currently a Junior Research Fellow of Wolfson College. She was educated in Kenya, Essex and Balliol College, Oxford, where she gained a BA, an M.Phil. and a doctorate in eighteenth-century travel writing. She has published articles and reviews on eighteenth-century literature and taught widely on literature of the seventeenth to nineteenth centuries.

SELECTED POEMS OF THOMAS GRAY, CHARLES CHURCHILL AND WILLIAM COWPER

Edited with an Introduction and Notes by
KATHERINE TURNER

PENGUIN BOOKS

PENGUIN BOOKS

Published by the Penguin Group
Penguin Books Ltd, 27 Wrights Lane, London w8 5tz, England
Penguin Books USA Inc., 375 Hudson Street, New York, New York 10014, USA
Penguin Books Australia Ltd, Ringwood, Victoria, Australia
Penguin Books Canada Ltd, 10 Alcorn Avenue, Toronto, Ontario, Canada m4v 3b2
Penguin Books (NZ) Ltd, 182–190 Wairau Road, Auckland 10, New Zealand

Penguin Books Ltd, Registered Offices: Harmondsworth, Middlesex, England

This edition first published 1997
10 9 8 7 6 5 4 3 2 1

Set in 10/11.5pt PostScript Monotype Ehrhardt
Typeset by Rowland Phototypesetting Ltd, Bury St Edmunds, Suffolk
Printed in England by Clays Ltd, St Ives plc

CONTENTS

INTRODUCTION

In 1816, after visiting a churchyard in Dover, Byron described how

> I stood beside the grave of him who blazed
> The comet of a season, and I saw
> The humblest of all sepulchres, and gazed
> With not the less of sorrow and of awe
> On that neglected turf and quiet stone,
> With name no clearer than the names unknown,
> Which lay unread around it . . .
>
> ('Churchill's Grave', lines 1–7)

The decline from fame into obscurity – 'The glory and the nothing of a name' – is the poem's central concern; its subject is the satiric poet and libertine priest, Charles Churchill (1731–64). Byron's poem also contains a rich tapestry of allusion to Thomas Gray's 'Elegy Written in a Country Churchyard' (1751), most poignantly to Gray's observation that 'The paths of glory lead but to the grave'. It is a peculiar moment in literary history, as two outspoken libertines and controversialists are yoked together through the elegiac moralizing of a famously reclusive scholar-poet. This strange conjunction opens up fresh perspectives on the poetic character of the mid to late eighteenth century. Whether labelled 'Pre-Romantic' or the 'Age of Sensibility', the years from the death of Pope in 1744 to the publication of *Lyrical Ballads* in 1798 tend to be characterized as elegiac and introspective, as reacting against the satiric engagement with public affairs of Pope and Swift, but without finding an alternative focus for poetry. However, as Byron's lines on Churchill suggest, and as this selection demonstrates, the thematic, formal and emotional variety of the 'Pre-Romantic' period – which, after all, laid foundations for poets as diverse as Coleridge and Byron – needs to be recognized. Even individually, the careers of Thomas Gray, Charles Churchill and William Cowper provide ample testimony

to the varied energies and directions of English poetry after Pope;
when they are read together, the evidence for English poetry's
resourcefulness and inventiveness at this time is every bit as com-
pelling as the old arguments for a period of poetic anxiety and
paralysis.

The frequent appearance of the grave itself, as a potent icon not
merely of mortality but in particular of poetic endeavour, has much
to do with the gloomy and defeatist image of mid-eighteenth-century
poetry. Gray is sometimes bracketed with the so-called 'graveyard
poets' of the 1740s and 1750s, such as Robert Blair and Edward
Young, respective authors of 'The Grave' (1743) and 'Night
Thoughts' (1742–6). But shortly after finishing the 'Elegy', Gray
himself mocks the reclusive poet of sensibility in the sly humour of
'A Long Story'. Similarly, for every line of Cowper's concerned
with death and damnation, and bolstering the image of the poet as
the 'stricken deer', there are probably ten concerned with the quick
of life. And when, in his poem 'The Candidate' (1764), Churchill
imagines the very scene which Byron is later to enact, it is with a
jesting air of robust epicureanism:

> Let one poor sprig of bay around my head
> Bloom whilst I live, and point me out when dead;
> Let it (may Heaven indulgent grant that prayer)
> Be planted on my grave, nor wither there;
> And when, on travel bound, some rhyming guest
> Roams through the churchyard, whilst his dinner's dressed,
> Let it hold up this comment to his eyes;
> Life to the last enjoyed, *here* Churchill lies;
> Whilst (Oh, what joy that pleasing flattery gives)
> Reading my works, he cries – *here* Churchill lives.

(lines 145–54)

It must be confessed, however, that to most twentieth-century
readers, Charles Churchill's works do not live. Indeed, as Byron
could have foreseen, few twentieth-century readers have probably
even heard of Churchill. There are obvious reasons for his obscurity.
He is an anthologist's nightmare, his poems habitually running to
many hundreds of lines; and his works are invariably topical, pro-
voked by moral and political issues brewed in the heady atmosphere

of London during the 1760s, and not necessarily addressing the universal concerns which are expected from real 'poetry'. Robert Southey, in his *Life of Cowper*, observes of Churchill, Cowper's old schoolfriend, that 'No English poet had ever enjoyed so excessive and so short-lived a popularity'. Southey goes on to observe that 'Cowper had a higher opinion of Churchill than of any other contemporary writer', and that Cowper made Churchill 'more than any other writer, his model'.[1] In 1780, Cowper declares in a letter that 'Churchill, the great Churchill, deserved the Name of Poet. Such natural unforced Effusions of Genius, the World I beleive has never seen since the Days of Shakespear'.[2] And in 'Table Talk', one of the 'moral satires' in rhyming couplets which Cowper published in his first volume of poetry in 1782, Churchill is presented as the sole spark of poetic wit and energy since the days of Pope and Swift. Cowper's description is carefully balanced between praise and censure: Churchill as a man and as a poet is both awe-inspiring and, we sense, fundamentally 'other' for the fastidious Cowper:

> Surly and slovenly, and bold and coarse,
> Too proud for art, and trusting in mere force,
> Spendthrift alike of money and of wit,
> Always at speed, and never drawing bit,
> He struck the lyre in such a careless mood,
> And so disdained the rules he understood,
> The laurel seemed to wait on his command;
> He snatched it rudely from the muses' hand.
>
> (lines 682–9)

But since Cowper's day, Churchill's voice – aggressively masculine, stridently self-confident – has been gradually silenced; his is not the voice we want our 'Pre-Romantic' poets to speak. We have cultivated instead an image of the Pre-Romantic poet as hesitant, self-questioning, effeminate and oblique; someone much like Thomas Gray, in fact, a poet who shunned publicity (refusing the Laureateship in 1757) and increasingly retreated not only from public life, but from the writing of poetry itself, into abstruse literary-historical researches at Cambridge, and a doomed infatuation with Charles-Victor de Bonstetten, a handsome and capricious young Swiss.

But this is only half of Gray's story. The shy recluse also travelled extensively in Europe and Britain; the poet who wrote the 'Elegy' also penned the humorous 'Ode on the Death of a Favourite Cat', as well as satiric poems responding to specific social and political events; and, of his and Churchill's poems on 'The Candidate', it is Gray's which is best remembered, and not just because Gray is the better-known poet. We should, moreover, recall that on Gray's death his friends Horace Walpole and William Mason (who was also his literary executor) destroyed many satirical poems in manuscript, with titles like 'A Character of the Scotch' and 'A History of Hell'.[3]

As early as 1771, it would seem, a particular image of the mid-eighteenth-century poet was being fashioned. And it was an image largely congenial to the eighteenth-century literati. Roger Lonsdale has documented the tide of enthusiasm which greeted Gray's *Odes* in 1757 – notwithstanding the perplexity to which many readers admitted (Boswell recalls remarking to Goldsmith that 'I have read his odes till I was almost mad', to which the saner Goldsmith replied 'They are terribly obscure'). By 1790 Joshua Reynolds was describing Gray as 'our great Lyrick Poet', and referring to 'his sublime idea of the indignant Welch bard'. As Lonsdale shows, Johnson's stern disapproval (in his 1781 *Life of Gray*, and in his conversation) of the *Odes*' self-conscious sublimity and difficulty was out of tune with much public opinion.[4]

Intriguingly, though, both Churchill and Cowper inclined to Johnson's view. Churchill on several occasions mocked Gray and William Mason as sickly lyricists, and his cronies Robert Lloyd and George Colman published skilful parodies of Gray's *Odes* in 1760 ('An Ode to Obscurity' and 'An Ode to Oblivion'), which Johnson admired. Even the mild-mannered William Cowper was moved to pen a parodic 'Dissertation on the Modern Ode', published in the *St James's Magazine* in June 1763. The dispute over the *Odes*, though, is only one aspect of the relationships between Gray, Churchill and Cowper. Robert Lloyd (Churchill's closest friend) admired the 'Elegy' so much that he translated it into Latin. As we know, both Churchill and Gray penned squibs (both entitled 'The Candidate') on the self-promoting Earl of Sandwich in 1764. Cowper, despite his early mockery of the *Odes*, clearly admired much of Gray's work; the echo of the 'Elegy' at the close of Book IV of *The Task* is telling, and Cowper also took inspiration from 'The Bard' when he wrote 'Boadicea, an Ode' in 1780–1. Perhaps most intriguingly of all, Gray made some detailed notes, with evident interest, on his two-volume edition of Churchill's *Works*; these notes are still valuable to editors today for their identification and explanation of Churchill's satiric targets.[5] These curious poetic and critical intersections highlight once more the varied and experimental energies of the time.

Where Churchill and Cowper most markedly part company with Gray (and the *Odes* controversy highlights this) is over the question of poetic language. In a letter to his friend Richard West which has become famous, Gray remarked that 'the language of the age is never the language of poetry', and his *oeuvre* as a whole prompted, and continues to fuel, frequent critical debate over poetic diction.[6] Samuel Johnson condemned the *Odes*' 'strutting dignity', while admiring the appeal of 'Elegy' to the 'common reader', observing that it 'abounds with images which find a mirror in every mind, and with sentiments to which every bosom returns an echo'.[7] Wordsworth, in his 1800 'Preface' to *Lyrical Ballads*, anatomizes Gray's 'Sonnet on the Death of Richard West' and rejects nine of its fourteen lines as defective because of their consciously poetic diction. The example of Gray is central to Wordsworth's deduction in his 1802 'Appendix' to the *Lyrical Ballads*, on poetic diction, that 'in proportion as ideas and feelings are valuable, whether the composition be in prose or verse, they require and exact one and the same language'.[8]

Wordsworth's views on poetic language had been anticipated by Cowper, who had observed in 1782 that

To make verse speak the language of prose, without being prosaic, to marshall the words of it in such an order, as they might naturally take in falling from the lips of an extemporary speaker, yet without meanness; harmoniously, elegantly, and without seeming to displace a syllable for the sake of the rhyme, is one of the most arduous tasks a poet can undertake.[9]

In Coleridge's opinion, Cowper himself attained this absolute mastery, and was one of the first poets who 'combined natural thoughts with natural diction', and 'reconciled the heart with the head'.[10] If this is true, then Cowper's achievement owes much to the lively controversies over poetry and language to which the careers of Gray and Churchill had contributed. Cowper acknowledges his stylistic debt to Churchill on several occasions, admiring for example the 'Strength and Spirit, & . . . that bold Masculine Character, which I think is the great Peculiarity of this Writer'.[11]

In terms of poetic language, then, a web of agreement and contradiction between Gray, Churchill and Cowper begins to take shape. Formally, too, affinity and difference co-exist. Churchill is the least varied and experimental of the three in formal terms. His poems, with rare exceptions such as 'The Crab', which he did not publish, unfold in an urgent monologue of rhyming couplets, more like Dryden than Pope in their vigour, but occasionally – as in 'The Conference' – employing the Popeian device of dialogue and philosophical debate. Churchill's argument is generally advanced with vehemence, passion, contempt and wit; the poet's moral independence is urged vociferously, and the role of reason is consciously downplayed (an important instance of what we tend now to see as a 'Romantic' posture). Gray's most pointed, and most political, satires ('The Candidate'; 'On Lord Holland's Seat') are likewise expressed in rhyming couplets, although they do not depend upon an aggressively defined satiric persona. Gray's work as a whole is astonishing for its variety of formal experimentation within a comparatively small output. His approach is sophisticated, highly technical, acutely aware of poetic decorum even when flouting it. His output was small, but what he did write was in such a variety of modes that he never seemed fully to inhabit, or claim as his own, any particular poetic form. Poetry for Gray was always an intensely self-conscious and literary activity, whereas for Cowper it became as natural as thought itself: 'When I can find no other Occupation, I think, and when I think, I am very apt to do it in Rhime.'[12] Churchill, who produced a phenomenal amount of verse within a very few years, declares a similar facility of composition – 'In verse I talk by day, I dream by night' ('The Journey', l. 50) – which verges on compulsion.

As Thomas Lockwood has admirably shown, Churchill's work effects a crucial shift in emphasis from satire as a genre to satire as a 'certain sort of feeling'.[13] Cowper first presented himself to the public in, predominantly, this Churchillian mode, in the 'moral satires' of his 1782 volume of *Poems* (these are not represented here, but a similar satiric venture, 'Tirocinium', 1785, is). The 1782 volume also contained a miscellany of shorter poems, and Cowper in the 1780s and 1790s continued to expand his formal range. He developed in particular the infinitely flexible and accessible blank verse of *The Task* and 'Yardley Oak', a form which increasingly accommodates high seriousness, mock-heroic, sly wit, social compassion and a distinctive conversational intimacy which Coleridge was to take as his model for the 'conversation poems'. The famously digressive style of Cowper's blank verse derives partly from Churchill, for whom digression was, if not the soul of wit, then certainly (in Cowper's phrase) the spice of life.

Cowper's has been dubbed the 'poetry of the ordinary'.[14] His verse, frequently addressed to friends and family as well as to a larger public, is profoundly sociable. He has undoubtedly suffered from his reputation as Jane Austen's favourite poet, from his consistent morality (which endeared him to generations of nineteenth-century readers but which alienates modern ones), and from his intimate rather than sublime visions of the natural world. Hazlitt's image of the poet peering at nature 'over his clipped hedges, and from his well-swept garden-walks' is as memorable as it is unjust.[15] The same is true of Byron's splenetic reference to 'that maniacal Calvinist & coddled poet'.[16] It is only perhaps within the past fifteen years that Cowper's significance has been properly reassessed. The work of Vincent Newey in particular has effectively repositioned Cowper at the heart of late eighteenth-century poetry, showing him to be a poet thoroughly responsive to politics and society, as well as the unassuming prophet of an emerging and revolutionary vision of nature as a 'showing forth' of God.

Formally, linguistically and tonally, then, the work of Gray, Churchill and Cowper presents an impressive variety as well as a network of coincidences and contradictions. Yet this would not in itself justify their yoking together in a selection of this nature. What further emerges from a reading of these poets in mutual relationship is the great range of concerns which their works share. All three are aware – with varying degrees of enthusiasm – that the transformation of literature into a commodity (a process whose beginnings Pope had surveyed with alarm) has now become a fact of life. Poethood is becoming a public profession. Churchill eagerly assumes the role created by Pope of the dissident, indignant poet, compelled to lash public vice and, increasingly, to publicize his personal integrity.

For Churchill as for Pope, the posture of satiric outrage proved fortunately lucrative: his attack on the London stage, 'The Rosciad' (1761), made Churchill famous overnight and wealthy enough to indulge his enjoyment of wine and women to a suicidal degree. Gray, by contrast, shrank from publicity, publishing little and that reluctantly. His rejection of the Laureateship and his scholarly retreat in Cambridge evince a disdain for the commercialization of poetry so intense that it shrivelled his creative impulses. For Cowper, moved increasingly to retreat from modern society through his own timidity and melancholia, poetry became not merely a means of communication with friends and family, but a vital connection with the wider world of social and political controversy, and a moral justification for his otherwise unproductive life. Especially in Cowper's work, grounded in the Buckinghamshire village of Olney, we see a growing challenge to the literary centrality of London in the eighteenth century. Even Churchill, in many ways the most urban of poets, describes a turning away from the city, not necessarily towards any alternative location, but towards a more subjective realm. Both Gray and Cowper can certainly be seen as anti-metropolitan as well as self-reflexive.

Another shared concern of these poets is the nature of their poetic inheritance, and their own place within the evolution of British poetry as well as within contemporary society. Gray's web of allusion to Spenser, Shakespeare and Milton, as well as to more recent poets and ancient poetic models, insistently highlights the disorientation of modern poetry, in 'this benighted age': 'Oh! lyre divine, what daring spirit / Wakes thee now?' is a question that remains unanswered in 'The Bard'. Churchill frequently outlines his own poetic genealogy (as in the closing stanzas of 'The Apology'), presenting a more confident view of his own abilities than does Gray, and celebrating the generous gifts of reason, conviction, and love of justice bestowed on him, 'The friend of virtue and the guide to truth' ('The Apology', line 415).

Increasingly, too, Churchill acknowledges the isolation to which the poet is susceptible; 'I on my journey all alone proceed' may have been the last line he penned. For Cowper, the loneliness of the virtuous was a condition of life rather than poethood; from his poetic inheritance itself, he seems to have derived strength and a sense of belonging. His most powerful debt is to Milton, who provided him with the highest ideals of personal integrity, and a verse form that could accommodate high seriousness as well as light pastiche and mock heroic.

An interest in childhood, education and environment is another preoccupation shared by Gray, Churchill and Cowper, most evident in Gray's 'Ode on a Distant Prospect of Eton College' and Cowper's 'Tirocinium', which conjures vivid scenes of the kind of schooling Cowper and Churchill received at Westminster. This interest in boyhood and the process of growing up relates to a concern with sexuality and self-confidence; the nature of masculinity and its relationship to virtue is scrutinized by all three poets, although Churchill's aggressive heterosexuality (carried to homophobic extremes in 'The Times') contrasts markedly with the sexual ambivalence of both Gray and Cowper (the latter apparently came to believe, after about 1763, that he was a hermaphrodite, although this conviction probably owed more to religious guilt and depression than to biology).[17]

Politically, Gray, Churchill and Cowper are all broadly Whiggish, defending English traditions of poetic and political liberty. Churchill, with his propagandist involvement with John Wilkes in the 1760s, is the most politically active of the three poets; but Cowper's poetry repeatedly comments on issues such as colonization, slavery, empire, poverty and cruelty to animals. Gray's apparently abstruse interest in ancient British poetry is part of a patriotic and Whiggish programme of national freedom and eminence. Above all, perhaps, what links these poets is their profound concern with the nature of poetry, the role of the poet, and the future of the nation; and, beyond all this, the insignificance of private and public concerns alike in the face of infinity and oblivion. But the range and continuing vitality of their work testifies to their engagement with, rather than retreat from, these concerns.

Notes

1. Robert Southey, *The Works of William Cowper* (15 vols., London, 1835–7), i, 83; 87–8.
2. To William Unwin, probably in March 1780; James King and Charles

Ryskamp, eds., *The Letters and Prose Writings of William Cowper* (5 vols., Oxford, 1979–86), i, 319.

3. See the correspondence between Walpole and Mason in *Horace Walpole's Correspondence*, ed. W. S. Lewis (48 vols., Oxford, 1937–83), xxviii, 76; 165–6.

4. Roger Lonsdale, 'Gray and Johnson: The Biographical Problem', in James Downey and Ben Jones, eds., *Fearful Joy* (Montreal and London, 1974), 66–84.

5. See Edmund Gosse, 'Gray's Notes on Churchill', *Transactions of the Royal Society of Literature*, 2nd series, 36 (1918), 161–79.

6. Letter to West, 8 April 1742; Paget Toynbee and Leonard Whibley, eds., *Correspondence of Thomas Gray* (3 vols., Oxford, 1971), i, 192.

7. 'Thomas Gray', in *Lives of the English Poets* (London, 1779–81; repr. 2 vols., 1964–5), ii, 392.

8. See Wordsworth and Coleridge, *Lyrical Ballads* (1798), ed. R. L. Brett and A. R. Jones (London and New York, 1963; repr. 1988), 252–3; 318.

9. Letter to William Unwin, 17 January 1782; *Letters and Prose Writings* (1979–86), ii, 10.

10. *Biographia Literaria* (1817), ed. James Engell and Walter Jackson Bate (2 vols., Princeton, 1983), i, 25.

11. Letter to Unwin, probably March 1780; *Letters and Prose Writings*, i, 320.

12. Letter to Joseph Hill, 9 May 1781; *Letters and Prose Writings*, i, 470.

13. Thomas Lockwood, *Post-Augustan Satire: Charles Churchill and Satirical Poetry, 1750–1800* (Seattle and London, 1979), 31–2 and *passim*.

14. W. B. Hutchings, *The Poetry of William Cowper* (London, 1983), 13.

15. 'On Thomson and Cowper', from *Lectures on the English Poets*, in *The Complete Works of William Hazlitt*, ed. P. P. Howe (21 vols., London and Toronto, 1930–4), v, 91–2.

16. Letter to John Murray, 20 May 1820, in *Byron's Letters and Journals*, ed. Leslie A. Marchand (12 vols., London, 1973–82), vii, 101.

17. See James King, *William Cowper: A Biography* (Durham, NC, 1986), 28.

TABLE OF DATES

Unless indicated to the contrary, reference is to date of publication, not composition, of literary works.

1716 (26 December) THOMAS GRAY born in Cornhill, London, son of Philip Gray, scrivener, and Dorothy, the only child of twelve to survive.

1717 David Garrick born. Horace Walpole born.

1719 Daniel Defoe, *Robinson Crusoe*. Joseph Addison dies.

1720 South Sea Bubble and Bill. War with Spain (until 1729).

1721 William Collins born. Mark Akenside born. Tobias Smollett born.

1722 Christopher Smart born. Joseph Warton born.

1722–42 Robert Walpole's Whig oligarchy in power.

1723 Adam Smith born.

1724 Bonnell Thornton born.

1726 Jonathan Swift, *Gulliver's Travels*. James Thomson, 'Winter'.

c. 1725–34 Gray at Eton. Befriends Horace Walpole, Richard West, and Thomas Ashton; this group call themselves the Quadruple Alliance.

1727 George I dies and George II accedes. John Gay's *Fables*, I (II in 1738). Thomson, 'Summer'. Isaac Newton dies. John Wilkes born.

1728 Alexander Pope, *Dunciad*, I–III (IV in 1743). Thomson, 'Spring'. Gay, *Beggar's Opera*. Thomas Warton (junior) born.

1729 Thomson, *Britannia*. Swift, *Modest Proposal*. Richard Steele dies. William Congreve dies. Edmund Burke born. Thomas Percy born.

1730 Thomson, *The Seasons* (with 'Autumn'). Oliver Goldsmith born.

1731 (February) CHARLES CHURCHILL born in Vine Street, Westminster, son of Charles Churchill, curate and lecturer of St John the Evangelist, Westminster (later also rector of

Rainham, Essex), and Ann. (15 November) WILLIAM COWPER born in the rectory, Berkhamsted, Hertfordshire, son of the Revd John Cowper, and Ann.

1731–8   Pope, *Epistles* and *Imitations of Horace*.

1732   Gay dies. George Colman born.

1733   Joseph Priestley born. Robert Lloyd born.

1734   (4 July) Gray enters Peterhouse, Cambridge, as a pensioner; is admitted fully on 9 October. Ashton and Walpole enter King's College, Cambridge, in 1734 (but West matriculates at Christ Church, Oxford, in May 1735).

1735   (22 November) Gray admitted at the Inner Temple in London. Thomson, *Liberty*, I–III. John Arbuthnot dies. James Beattie born.

1736   Gin Act. Porteous Riots. (12 February) Gray inherits small property from his aunt Sarah. Thomson, *Liberty*, IV–V and complete. James Macpherson born.

1737   Death of Cowper's mother Ann. Edward Gibbon born.

c. 1737–42   Cowper attends various schools in Hertfordshire and Bedfordshire.

1738   (14 September) Gray leaves Cambridge, returns to father's house, intended for the law. Samuel Johnson, *London*. Pope, 'Epilogue to the Satires'.

1739   (29 March) Gray begins Grand Tour with Walpole. Swift, 'Verses on the Death of Dr Swift'. David Hume, *Treatise of Human Nature* (concluded 1740).

1740   War of Austrian Succession begins. Samuel Richardson, *Pamela*. James Boswell born.

1741   (May–September) Gray quarrels with Walpole and returns to England after visiting the Grande Chartreuse (May) Churchill, aged nine, enters Westminster School. (November) Gray's father dies, leaving the family financially insecure.

c. 1741–8   Churchill at Westminster School. Befriends George Colman, William Cowper, Robert Lloyd, Bonnell Thornton.

1742   (April) Cowper enters Westminster School. (1 June) Death of Richard West, to whom Gray had just sent 'Ode on the Spring'. (August) Gray writes 'Sonnet on West', 'Eton Ode', 'Ode to Adversity'. (15 October) Gray returns to Peterhouse as a Fellow-commoner, and resides permanently at Cambridge from now on. (December) Gray's mother and aunt retire to

Stoke Poges. Collins, *Persian Eclogues*. Edward Young, *The Complaint, or Night-Thoughts* (concluded 1746).

1743 (October) Gray graduates as Bachelor of Laws. Robert Blair, *The Grave*. Pope, *The Dunciad* (final version).

1744 Akenside, *Pleasures of Imagination*. Pope dies.

1745 Jacobite rebellion. (8 November) Gray and Walpole reconciled. Churchill becomes King's Scholar at Westminster. Swift dies.

1746 Jacobite rebellion crushed at Culloden. Collins, *Odes*. Joseph Warton, *Odes on Various Subjects*.

1747 Gray's 'Ode on Eton College' published by Dodsley. Thomas Warton, *Pleasures of Melancholy*. Richardson, *Clarissa* (concluded 1748).

1748 (15 January) Dodsley's *Collection of Poems*, vols. I–III, including Gray's 'Ode to Spring' and 'On the Death of a Favourite Cat'. (January or February) Gray befriends William Mason. (25 March) Gray's house in Cornhill burned down. (29 April) Cowper admitted to the Middle Temple. (8 July) Churchill, aged sixteen, enrols as student at St John's College, Cambridge; soon leaves for obscure reasons. Thornton, Colman and Lloyd go to Oxford. Thomson dies; his *Castle of Indolence* published.

1749 Churchill runs off with, and secretly marries, Martha Scott: prepares to become a clergyman. Collins, 'On the Death of Thomson' and 'The Passions'. Johnson, *The Vanity of Human Wishes*. Henry Fielding, *Tom Jones*. *Monthly Review* (to 1845).

1750 (12 June) Gray sends 'Elegy' to Walpole; it passes into manuscript circulation. (August–September) Gray writes 'A Long Story'.

1750–3 Cowper articled to a London solicitor, and spends much time with his cousins, Theadora and Harriet Cowper.

1751 Churchill and Martha move to Sunderland, he pursues his studies for the church. (15 February) Gray's 'Elegy' published by Dodsley.

1752 Thomas Chatterton born.

1752–7 Gray writes 'The Bard' and 'The Progress of Poesy'.

1753 Hardwicke's Marriage Act. Churchill and Martha return to Westminster. (11 March) Gray's mother dies. (29 March)

Gray's *Six Poems with Designs by Mr. Bentley*. (November) Cowper's first period of depression.

c. 1753–4   Cowper abandons hope of marrying his cousin Theadora Cowper.

1754   Anglo-French hostilities begin in North America. (June) Cowper called to the Bar. (22 November) Churchill ordained deacon. Thomas Warton, *Observations on the Faerie Queene*. Fielding dies. George Crabbe born.

1754–6   Churchill a poor curate at South Cadbury and Sparkford in Somerset. Writes early drafts of 'The Ghost'. Colman and Thornton produce magazine *The Connoisseur*, 1754–6, to which Cowper contributes some essays.

1755   The Nonsense Club formed in London, led by Thornton and including Colman, Lloyd, Cowper and perhaps Churchill. Jean-Jacques Rousseau's *Discourse on Inequality*. Fielding's *Journal of a Voyage to Lisbon*. Johnson's *Dictionary*.

1756   Outbreak of Seven Years War with France. (5 March) Gray moves from Peterhouse to Pembroke Hall. (19 December) Churchill ordained priest; takes over his father's curacy at Rainham in Essex, and moves wife and two sons there. Death of Cowper's father. William Mason, *Odes*. Joseph Warton, *Essay on the Writings and Genius of Pope* (II in 1782). *Critical Review* (to 1817).

1757   John Wilkes elected MP for Aylesbury. (15 April) Cowper admitted to the Inner Temple. (8 August) Gray's *Odes* published, printed at Strawberry Hill Press. (5 December) Gray declines the Poet Laureateship. Burke, *A Philosophical Enquiry into . . . the Sublime and Beautiful*. William Blake born.

1758   (June) Churchill may have met John Wilkes, then churchwarden of St Margaret's, Westminster. (7 September) Churchill's father dies; Churchill inherits the curacy and lectureship of St John's in Westminster, and moves there but has financial troubles. Tutors in English at Mrs Dennis's Boarding School for Girls in Bloomsbury, and deepens acquaintance with Wilkes.

1759   (9 March) Churchill's daughter Charlotte born. Churchill and Martha living separately. Johnson, *Rasselas*. Adam Smith, *Theory of Moral Sentiments*. Edward Young, *Conjectures on*

Original Composition. Collins dies. Robert Burns born. Mary Wollstonecraft born.

1760 George II dies, George III accedes. Churchill bankrupted; rescued from debtors' prison by Lloyd's father (whom he later thanks in 'The Conference'). (April) Robert Lloyd's poem 'The Actor' appears. Lloyd and Colman burlesque Gray and Mason in 'An Ode to Obscurity' and 'An Ode to Oblivion'. Macpherson, *Fragments of Ancient Poetry* (which Gray reads with enthusiasm). Laurence Sterne, *Tristram Shandy*, vols. I and II (and successive volumes to 1767). William Beckford born.

1761 William Pitt resigns. (14 March) Churchill's 'The Rosciad'. Churchill reaps large profits; leads an increasingly debauched life. (May) Churchill's 'The Apology', an attack on the reviews. By May, Gray has written 'The Fatal Sisters', 'The Descent of Odin', and other imitations of Welsh and Norse poetry, intending to include them in his 'History of English Poetry', which he had first projected in 1752. (November) Churchill's 'Night', a celebration of the dissipated lifestyle. Richardson dies.

1762 (March) Books I and II of Churchill's *The Ghost*, a satire on popular superstitions. (5 June) *The North Briton* begins publication, edited and written by Wilkes, with Churchill's help. Its title satirizes that of Smollett's pro-ministry organ, *The Briton*, and its target is the Tory ministry of Lord Bute, George III's widely disliked Scots chief minister. (By September) Churchill has syphilis. (October) Book III of Churchill's *The Ghost*. (November) Gray fails to obtain Regius Professorship of Modern History at Cambridge. Johnson receives royal pension. Macpherson's *Fingal*. Rousseau's *Social Contract* and *Emile*. Lady Mary Wortley Montagu dies. William Bowles born. William Cobbett born.

1763 Peace of Paris ends Seven Years' War with France. Cowper mocks Gray and Mason in 'A Dissertation on the Modern Ode', published in the *St James's Magazine* for April. Cowper summoned to appear at the Bar of the House of Lords and makes third suicide attempt; beginning of his second period of depression. Enters mental asylum at St Albans. (January) Churchill's 'The Prophecy of Famine', a satire against the

Scots and Bute. Churchill resigns as curate of St John's, Westminster. (8 April) Bute resigns as first minister; succeeded by Grenville. (23 April) *The North Briton* No. 45 appears; Wilkes is arrested on charges of sedition and blasphemy, prompting violent and lasting controversy ('Wilkes and Liberty') over the legality of general warrants. (June) Churchill, 'Epistle to William Hogarth', attacking Hogarth's talents and Tory politics. (October or November) Churchill elopes with fifteen-year-old Elizabeth Carr. (15 November) Wilkes's *Essay on Woman* is denounced in House of Lords; in House of Commons, *North Briton* 45 is pronounced a 'seditious libel'. Wilkes fights a duel with one of his accusers, Samuel Martin. (Also in November) Churchill, 'The Conference' and Book IV of *The Ghost*. (December) Churchill, 'The Author'. (24 December) Wilkes flees to exile in France to avoid arrest. Macpherson, *Tamora*. Christopher Smart, *Song to David*.

1764 (19 January) Wilkes expelled, in his absence, from House of Commons. (January) Churchill, 'The Duellist' (on Wilkes's duel with Samuel Martin). (February, March, August) Churchill's miscellaneous fantasy, *Gotham*. (January–March) Gray writes 'The Candidate', a satiric attack on the Earl of Sandwich's application for the High Stewardship of Cambridge University. (May) Churchill's own attack on Sandwich, 'The Candidate'. (June) Churchill, 'The Farewell'. (July) Cowper begins mental recovery and conversion to evangelicalism. (September) Churchill, 'The Times'. (October) Churchill, 'Independence'. (22 October) Churchill leaves London for Boulogne to join Wilkes in France; seized by fever (possibly typhus) on 29 October. (1 November) Wilkes outlawed for failing to appear at the court of King's Bench. (4 November) Churchill dies suddenly, aged thirty-three, in Wilkes's arms, at Boulogne. Conveyed to Dover and buried. (4 December) Robert Lloyd dies. Goldsmith, 'The Traveller'. Hogarth dies. Ann Radcliffe born.

1764–6 Gray travels around England and Scotland.

1765 (February) Churchill's *Sermons* published by the poet's brother John, including the satiric verse 'Dedication' to Bishop

Warburton of Gloucester. (April) Churchill, 'The Journey' (unfinished at his death). (June) Cowper leaves St Albans; lodges in Huntingdon. (*c.* September) Cowper makes acquaintance of Unwin family. (11 November) Cowper becomes a boarder with Unwin family. Percy, *Reliques of Ancient English Poetry*. Johnson, edition of *Shakespeare*. Walpole, *The Castle of Otranto*. Edward Young dies.

1766 Goldsmith, *The Vicar of Wakefield*. Smollett, *Travels through France and Italy*.

1767 Increasing tax pressure on American colonies under Townshend's ministry. (2 July) Death of the Revd Morley Unwin. (14 September) Cowper and Mrs Unwin move to Olney, where the Revd John Newton had offered to find them a house. Maria Edgeworth born.

1768 Wilkes returns to England and is sentenced for libel. Cowper and Mrs Unwin move into Orchard Side, Olney. (12 March) Gray's collected *Poems*. (June) Gray writes 'On Lord Holland's Seat at Margate'. (July) Gray appointed Regius Professor of Modern History at Cambridge. Sterne, *Sentimental Journey*.

1769 Wilkes expelled from Commons and re-elected three times. Riots and bloodshed in his support, St George's Field massacre, 5 May. Shakespeare Jubilee at Stratford-on-Avon. Chatterton, 'Elinoure and Juga'.

1770 Death of Cowper's brother John. Goldsmith, 'The Deserted Village'. Akenside dies. Chatterton dies. Sterne dies. James Hogg born. William Wordsworth born.

1771 (30 July) Gray dies at Cambridge. Buried at Stoke Poges. Cowper begins *Olney Hymns*, in collaboration with Newton. Beattie, 'The Minstrel'. Henry Mackenzie, *The Man of Feeling*. Smollett, *Humphry Clinker*. Thomas Pennant, *Tour in Scotland*. Smart dies. Smollett dies. Walter Scott born.

1772 Cowper engaged to Mrs Unwin. Samuel Taylor Coleridge born.

1773 Boston 'tea party'. Cowper's engagement to Mrs Unwin broken; third period of serious depression. (April) Cowper moves to Olney vicarage, under Newton's care. (October) Cowper makes suicide attempt. Goldsmith, *She Stoops to*

Conquer. John Hawkesworth, *Account of the Voyages undertaken in the Southern Hemisphere* (Cook's voyages). James Mill born.

1774 First Congress of American colonies. (23 May) Cowper returns to Orchard Side in Olney. Thomas Warton, *History of English Poetry* (concluded 1781). Johann Wolfgang von Goethe, *Sorrows of Young Werther*. Goldsmith dies. Robert Southey born.

1774–5 Wilkes elected Lord Mayor of London and returned to Parliament; opposes taxation of American colonies.

1775 Battles of Lexington, Concord, and Bunker Hill in American war. Mason's edition of Gray, with *Life*. Johnson, *Taxation no Tyranny* and *Journey to the Western Islands of Scotland*. Richard Brinsley Sheridan, *The Rivals*. Crabbe, *Inebriety*. Jane Austen born. Charles Lamb born. Walter Savage Landor born. Matthew Lewis born.

1776 American Declaration of Independence. Gibbon, *Decline and Fall of the Roman Empire* (completed 1789). Adam Smith, *Wealth of Nations*. Hume dies.

1777 Boswell, *The Hypochondriack* (to 1783). Chatterton, *Poems . . . by Rowley*. Thomas Warton, *Poems*.

1778 Death of Pitt. French-American alliance; Britain declares war on France. Rousseau dies. Voltaire dies. William Hazlitt born.

1779 War with Spain. Johnson's *Prefaces to . . . English Poets* completed 1781. Cowper and Newton, *Olney Hymns*.

1780 Gordon Riots. Cowper begins to write his 'moral essays'. Crabbe, 'The Candidate'.

1781 Cornwallis capitulates at Yorktown. (July) Cowper meets Lady Austen. Crabbe, 'The Library'. Immanuel Kant, *Critique of Pure Reason*. Rousseau, *Confessions*.

1782 Lord North's ministry falls. Cowper, *Poems*; and writes 'John Gilpin'. Thomas Warton, 'Verses on Reynolds' Painted Window'. Gilpin, *Observations on the River Wye*. Choderlos Laclos, *Les Liaisons Dangereuses*.

1783 Fox–North coalition, then Pitt the Younger's first ministry. Peace of Versailles with France. (*c.* October) Cowper begins *The Task*. Blake, *Poetical Sketches*. Crabbe, *The Village*. Beckford, *Dreams, Waking Thoughts, and Incidents*.

1784 Pitt's India Act. Cowper meets the Throckmortons. (May–July) Cowper's final breach with Lady Austen. (October) Cowper completes *The Task*. (November) Cowper completes 'Tirocinium' and begins translating the *Iliad*. Johnson dies. Diderot dies. Leigh Hunt born.

1785 Warren Hastings returns from India. Thomas Warton becomes Poet Laureate. (July) Cowper, *The Task*. (October) Cowper resumes correspondence with Lady Hesketh, and receives financial assistance from her and (anonymously) Theadora. Crabbe, *The Newspaper*. Boswell, *Tour to the Hebrides*. Clara Reeve, *The Progress of Romance*. Thomas Love Peacock born. Thomas De Quincey born.

1786 (November) Cowper moves to The Lodge, Weston Underwood, at the invitation of the Throckmortons. Beckford, *Vathek*. William Gilpin, *Observations on the Mountains and Lakes of Cumberland*. Hester Piozzi, *Anecdotes of Johnson*.

1787 United States Constitution signed. Association for Abolition of the Slave Trade begins. (January–June) Cowper's fourth period of depression. Wollstonecraft, *Thoughts on the Education of Daughters*.

1788 Trial of Warren Hastings begins. George III's first bout of madness. Cowper begins translation of the *Odyssey*. Collins, 'Ode on the Popular Superstitions of the Highlands'. Charles Wesley dies. George Gordon Byron born.

1789 Fall of the Bastille and Declaration of the Rights of Man. George III recovers. Blake, *Songs of Innocence* and *Book of Thel*. Bowles, *Sonnets*. Gilpin, *Observations on the Highlands of Scotland*. Radcliffe, *Castles of Athlin and Dunbayne*.

1790 Cowper makes acquaintance of his cousin, John Johnson. Burke, *Reflections on the Revolution in France*. Radcliffe, *A Sicilian Romance*. Wollstonecraft, *Vindication of the Rights of Men*.

1791 Priestley's home wrecked by mob in Birmingham. Louis XVI captured after the flight to Varennes. (July) Cowper's translation of Homer published. (September) Cowper begins translation of Milton's Latin and Italian poems. (December) Mrs Unwin's first paralytic stroke. Boswell, *Life of Johnson*. Thomas Paine, *Rights of Man* (II in 1792). Radcliffe, *The Romance of the Forest*. Joseph Ritson, *Ancient Popular Poetry*.

1792 Hastings acquitted. Continental allies invade France. French royal family imprisoned, and September massacres; Wordsworth in France. (May) Mrs Unwin's second paralytic stroke; and Cowper's first visit from William Hayley. (August–September) Cowper, Mrs Unwin and John Johnson visit Hayley at Eartham in Sussex. (Autumn) Cowper's depression returns. Wollstonecraft, *Vindication of the Rights of Woman*. Joshua Reynolds dies. Percy Bysshe Shelley born.

1793 (21 January) Execution of Louis XVI. (1 February) France declares war on Britain. The Terror; murder of Marat; execution of Marie Antoinette. (Autumn) Mrs Unwin continues to deteriorate; Cowper writes 'To Mary'. (November) Lady Hesketh arrives to supervise Cowper household. Blake, *Visions of the Daughters of Albion* and *America*. William Godwin, *Political Justice*. Wordsworth, 'An Evening Walk' and 'Descriptive Sketches'.

1794 Trial of Horne Tooke, Holcroft, Thelwall. Execution of Danton (April) and Robespierre (July). The Directorate. (January) Beginning of Cowper's final serious depression, from which he never fully recovers. (April) Cowper granted a yearly pension of £300. (17 May) Mrs Unwin's third paralytic stroke. Blake, *Songs of Experience*; *Europe*; *Book of Urizen*. Godwin, *Caleb Williams*. Uvedale Price, *Essay on the Picturesque*. Radcliffe, *Mysteries of Udolpho*.

1795 Food scarce and expensive after bad summer. Seditious Meetings Act and Treasonable Practices Act. (28 July) Cowper and Mrs Unwin removed by John Johnson to his house at East Dereham in Norfolk. Blake, *Book of Los* and *Ahania*. Lewis, *The Monk*. Boswell dies. John Keats born. Thomas Carlyle born.

1796 Napoleon Bonaparte's successful campaign in Italy. (17 December) Death of Mrs Unwin. Burke, *Letter to a Noble Lord* and *Letters on a Regicide Peace*. Coleridge, *Poems on Several Subjects*. Burns dies. Macpherson dies.

1797 Mutinies at Spithead and the Nore. Battles of Cape St Vincent and Camperdown. Cowper begins to revise the Homer translations. Radcliffe, *The Italian*. Southey, *Poems*. Burke dies. Walpole dies. Wollstonecraft dies.

1798 Irish rebellion. Switzerland invaded by France. France in

Syria and Egypt. Nelson in the Mediterranean. Coleridge, 'Fears in Solitude', 'France, an Ode' and 'Frost at Midnight'. Godwin, *Memoirs* of Wollstonecraft. Landor, *Gebir*. Thomas Malthus, *Principles of Population*. Wollstonecraft (post-humously), *Maria, or the Wrongs of Woman*. Wordsworth and Coleridge, *Lyrical Ballads*.

1799 Repression of radical groups such as Corresponding Society. Combination Acts against formation of unions. Fall of the Directorate in France; Bonaparte made First Consul. (8 March) Cowper completes revisions of Homer translations. (19 March) Cowper begins 'The Castaway'. Thomas Campbell, *The Pleasures of Hope*.

1800 Act of Union with Ireland. Battles of Alexandria and Marengo. (January and February) Cowper ailing. (25 April) Cowper dies. (2 May) Cowper buried in parish church of East Dereham. Edgeworth, *Castle Rackrent*. Wordsworth, *Preface to Lyrical Ballads*. Joseph Warton dies.

FURTHER READING

Thomas Gray

Editions

Gray, Collins and Goldsmith: The Complete Poems, ed. Roger Lonsdale
(London, 1969) (modernized text; fully annotated)

Thomas Gray and William Collins: Poetical Works, ed. Roger Lons-
dale (Oxford, 1977) (unmodernized text)

Correspondence of Thomas Gray, ed. Paget Toynbee and Leonard
Whibley, with Corrections and Additions by Herbert W. Starr
(3 vols., Oxford, 1971)

Bibliography

McKenzie, Alan T., Thomas Gray: A Reference Guide (Boston,
1982)

Northrup, Clark Sutherland, A Bibliography of Thomas Gray (New
Haven and Oxford, 1917)

Starr, Herbert W., A Bibliography of Thomas Gray 1917–1951
(Philadelphia, 1953)

Biography

Ketton-Cramer, R. W., Thomas Gray: A Biography (Cambridge,
1955)

Lytton-Sells, A. L., Thomas Gray: His Life and Works (London,
1980)

Criticism

Bloom, Harold, and Frederick W. Hilles, eds., From Sensibility to
Romanticism (New York, 1965); essays by Frank Brady, B. H.
Bronson and Ian Jack

Downey, James, and Ben Jones, eds., *Fearful Joy: Papers from the Thomas Gray Bicentenary Conference at Carleton University* (Montreal and London, 1974)

Hutchings, W. B., and William Ruddick, eds., *Thomas Gray: Contemporary Essays* (Liverpool, 1993)

Kaul, Suvir, *Thomas Gray and Literary Authority: A Study in Ideology and Poetics* (Stanford, CA, 1992)

Lonsdale, Roger, 'The Poetry of Thomas Gray: Versions of the Self' (Chatterton Lecture, British Academy, 1973)

Starr, Herbert W., ed., *Twentieth-Century Interpretations of Gray's Elegy: A Collection of Critical Essays* (Englewood Cliffs, NJ, 1968)

Charles Churchill

Edition

The Poetical Works of Charles Churchill, ed. Douglas Grant (Oxford, 1956)

Biography

Brown, Wallace Cable, *Charles Churchill: Poet, Rake, and Rebel* (New York, 1953; repr. 1968)

Criticism

Bertelson, Lance, *The Nonsense Club: Literature and Popular Culture, 1749–1764* (Oxford, 1986)

Golden, Morris, 'Churchill's Literary Influence on Cowper', *Journal of English and Germanic Philology*, 58 (1959), 655–65

Golden, Morris, 'Sterility and Eminence in the Poetry of Charles Churchill', *Journal of English and Germanic Philology*, 66 (1967), 333–46

Hatch, Ronald B., 'Charles Churchill and the Poetry of "Charter'd Freedom"', *English Studies in Canada*, 15/3 (September 1989), 277–87

Lockwood, Thomas F., *Post-Augustan Satire: Charles Churchill and Satirical Poetry* (Seattle and London, 1979)

Selden, Raman, *English Verse Satire 1590–1765* (London, 1978), 164–75

William Cowper

Editions

The Poems of William Cowper, ed. John D. Baird and Charles Ryskamp (3 vols., Oxford, 1980–95)

The Letters and Prose Writings of William Cowper, ed. James King and Charles Ryskamp (5 vols., Oxford, 1979–86)

The Task and Selected Other Poems, ed. James Sambrook (London and New York, 1994)

Bibliography

Dalrymple-Champneys, Norma, *A Bibliography of William Cowper to 1837* (Oxford, 1963)

Hartley, Lodwick, *William Cowper, the Continuing Revaluation: an Essay and a Bibliography of Cowperian Studies from 1895 to 1960* (Chapel Hill, NC, 1960)

Biography

King, James, *William Cowper: A Biography* (Durham, NC, 1986)

Ryskamp, Charles, *William Cowper of the Inner Temple, Esquire: A Study of his Life and Works to the Year 1768* (Cambridge, 1959); contains appendices of Cowper's minor prose writings

Criticism

Elfenbein, Andrew, 'Cowper's *Task* and the Anxieties of Femininity', *Eighteenth-Century Life*, 13/3 (1989), 1–17

Faulkner, Peter, 'William Cowper and the Poetry of Empire', *Durham University Journal*, new series, 52 (1991), 165–73

Feingold, Richard, *Nature and Society: Later Eighteenth-Century Uses of the Pastoral and Georgic* (Hassocks, Sussex, 1978)

Griffin, Dustin, 'Redefining Georgic: Cowper's *Task*', *Journal of English Literary History*, 57/4 (1990), 865–79

Hutchings, W. B., *The Poetry of William Cowper* (London, 1983)

Hutchings, W. B., 'William Cowper and 1789', *Yearbook of English Studies*, 19 (1989), 71–93

Newey, Vincent, *Cowper's Poetry: A Critical Study and Reassessment* (Liverpool, 1982)

Newey, Vincent, 'William Cowper and the Condition of England', in Vincent Newey and Ann Thompson, eds., *Literature and Nationalism* (Liverpool, 1991), 120–39

Nicholson, Norman, *William Cowper* (London, 1951)

Priestman, Martin, *Cowper's Task: Structure and Influence* (Cambridge, 1983)

Spacks, Patricia Meyer, *The Poetry of Vision: Five Eighteenth-Century Poets* (Cambridge, Mass., 1967)

EDITORIAL NOTE

The textual origins of the poems presented in this selection are described in the Note on the Text preceding each poet's work. Some general editorial points are made here.

The use of italics, and initial capitalization of nouns, are both habits of the printing house which were dying out in the eighteenth century, and are much less common in Cowper than in Gray. Churchill, or his printer, was unusually profligate with italics and capitalization of nouns (entire words as well as initial letters), and in their original form his texts present a rather dense and hysterical aspect. In this, he is rather old-fashioned, at a time when printing conventions were moving rapidly towards an elimination of capitals except for proper names and personifications. Thus, italics and initial capitalization of nouns have been largely eliminated from this selection, except in the case of personification; here, however, there are some marginal cases (for example, is 'contemplation' in Gray's 'Elegy', line 95 – not capitalized by Gray – a personification or an activity?).

Spelling is modernized throughout this selection, but conscious archaisms such as 'murther' are retained. Contractions (e.g., 'ev'ry', 'pleas'd') have been expanded except where of real metrical import. Punctuation has been lightly modernized. Italics have been retained (or supplied) for titles of literary works, e.g. the reference to Smollett's *Regicide* in Churchill's 'The Apology', line 156.

For direct speech within poems, I have retained quotation marks at the beginning and end of the speech, but have departed from the eighteenth-century use of quotation marks at the beginning of each line of direct speech, except where the speech continues into a new stanza, in which a reminder quotation mark is retained. Printers' errors have been silently corrected, and line numbers have been supplied.

None of these three poets were greatly given to annotation; however, some of Gray's, and more occasionally still Cowper's, poems were glossed by their authors. In such cases, the poet's notes are given as footnotes to the text on the page, and are presented in unmodernized form. The editor's notes to the poems appear at the end of the volume.

THOMAS GRAY

Poems

A NOTE ON THE TEXT

The last edition of Gray's poems to appear in his lifetime was in 1768, *Poems by Mr. Gray*, published by Dodsley in London and Foulis in Glasgow. This edition in many cases represents Gray's final revisions – including the addition of footnotes to some poems – and is the most frequent source for the text in this selection. Some of the poems had earlier appeared in an impressive illustrated folio in 1753, *Designs by Mr. R. Bentley for Six Poems by Mr. T. Gray*; 'A Long Story' appears only in 1753, since Gray wished to suppress it from the later edition.

Some poems appeared only after Gray's death, in William Mason's *The Poems of Mr. Gray, to which are prefixed Memoirs of his Life and Writings*, 1775; the *Memoirs* and *Poems* are paginated separately, and some poems appear in the body of the *Memoirs* only. Mason's source for most poems, but not all, is Gray's manuscript Commonplace Book in three volumes, now in possession of Pembroke College, Cambridge. The Commonplace Book, rather than Mason, is the version preferred here.

Gray's notes to the poems are presented in unmodernized form. Square brackets indicate proper names left blank in the originals and, in the case of the notes, may contain editorial completions of Gray's own, sometimes rather casual, references.

The interested reader can experience the text of Gray's poems in its original, eighteenth-century format in Gray and Collins, *Poetical Works*, ed. Roger Lonsdale (Oxford, 1977). Lonsdale's edition of Gray, Collins and Goldsmith, *The Complete Poems* (London and New York, 1969) presents a modernized text and absolutely indispensable footnotes, charting the richly allusive territory of Gray's verse. The notes given in the present selection aim more simply to elucidate the context and meaning of each poem, but every reader should consult Lonsdale's scholarship (to which the present editor is greatly indebted) for a true appreciation of Gray's allusiveness.

Ode on the Spring

Lo! where the rosy-bosomed Hours,
Fair Venus' train, appear,
Disclose the long-expecting flowers,
And wake the purple year!
5   The Attic warbler pours her throat,
Responsive to the cuckoo's note,
The untaught harmony of spring:
While whispering pleasure as they fly,
Cool zephyrs through the clear blue sky
10   Their gathered fragrance fling.

Where'er the oak's thick branches stretch
A broader browner shade;
Where'er the rude and moss-grown beech
O'er-canopies the glade,[1]
15   Beside some water's rushy brink
With me the Muse shall sit, and think
(At ease reclined in rustic state)
How vain the ardour of the crowd,
How low, how little are the proud,
20   How indigent the great!

Still is the toiling hand of Care;
The panting herds repose:
Yet hark, how through the peopled air
The busy murmur glows!
25   The insect youth are on the wing,
Eager to taste the honeyed spring,
And float amid the liquid noon:[2]

---

1. ——a bank
O'ercanopied with luscious woodbine.
                    Shakesp. Mids. Night's Dream [II. i. 249–51].

2. 'Nare per aestatem liquidam——'
                    Virgil. Georg. lib. 4. [line 59].

Some lightly o'er the current skim,
Some show their gaily-gilded trim
30   Quick-glancing to the sun.[3]

To Contemplation's sober eye[4]
Such is the race of man:
And they that creep, and they that fly,
Shall end where they began.
35   Alike the busy and the gay
But flutter through life's little day,
In fortune's varying colours dressed:
Brushed by the hand of rough Mischance,
Or chilled by age, their airy dance
40   They leave, in dust to rest.

Methinks I hear in accents low
The sportive kind reply:
Poor moralist! and what art thou?
A solitary fly!
45   Thy joys no glittering female meets,
No hive hast thou of hoarded sweets,
No painted plumage to display:
On hasty wings thy youth is flown;
Thy sun is set, thy spring is gone –
50   We frolic, while 'tis May.

3. ——sporting with quick glance
Shew to the sun their waved coats drop'd with gold.
                    Milton's Paradise Lost, book 7. [lines 405–6].

4. While insects from the threshold preach, *&c.*
                    M. Green, *in* [*T*]*he Grotto* [line 57].
                    Dodsley's Miscellanies, Vol. V. *p.* 161.

Ode on a Distant Prospect of Eton College

'Άνθρωπος· ἱκανὴ πρόφασις εἰς τὸ δυστλχεῖν.

Menander

Ye distant spires, ye antique towers,
That crown the watery glade,
Where grateful Science still adores
Her Henry's[1] holy shade;
5   And ye, that from the stately brow
Of Windsor's heights the expanse below
Of grove, of lawn, of mead survey,
Whose turf, whose shade, whose flowers among
Wanders the hoary Thames along
10   His silver-winding way.

    Ah happy hills, ah pleasing shade,
Ah fields beloved in vain,
Where once my careless childhood strayed,
A stranger yet to pain!
15   I feel the gales, that from ye blow,
A momentary bliss bestow,
As waving fresh their gladsome wing,
My weary soul they seem to soothe,
And, redolent of joy and youth,[2]
20   To breathe a second spring.

    Say, Father Thames, for thou hast seen
Full many a sprightly race
Disporting on thy margent green
The paths of pleasure trace,
25   Who foremost now delight to cleave
With pliant arm thy glassy wave?

1. King Henry the Sixth, Founder of the College.

2. And bees their honey redolent of spring.
                 Dryden's Fables on the Pythag. System. [line 110].

The captive linnet which enthrall?
What idle progeny succeed
To chase the rolling circle's speed,
Or urge the flying ball?

While some on urgent business bent
Their murmuring labours ply
'Gainst graver hours, that bring constraint
To sweeten liberty:
Some bold adventurers disdain
The limits of their little reign,
And unknown regions dare descry:
Still as they run they look behind,
They hear a voice in every wind,
And snatch a fearful joy.

Gay hope is theirs by fancy fed,
Less pleasing when possessed;
The tear forgot as soon as shed,
The sunshine of the breast:
Their buxom health of rosy hue,
Wild wit, invention ever-new,
And lively cheer of vigour born;
The thoughtless day, the easy night,
The spirits pure, the slumbers light,
That fly the approach of morn.

Alas, regardless of their doom,
The little victims play!
No sense have they of ills to come,
Nor cares beyond today;
Yet see how all around 'em wait
The ministers of human fate,
And black Misfortune's baleful train!
Ah, show them where in ambush stand
To seize their prey the murtherous band!
Ah, tell them, they are men!

These shall the fury Passions tear,
The vultures of the mind,
Disdainful Anger, pallid Fear,
And Shame that skulks behind;
65 Or pining Love shall waste their youth,
Or Jealousy with rankling tooth,
That inly gnaws the secret heart,
And Envy wan, and faded Care,
Grim-visaged comfortless Despair,
70 And Sorrow's piercing dart.

Ambition this shall tempt to rise,
Then whirl the wretch from high,
To bitter Scorn a sacrifice,
And grinning Infamy.
75 The stings of Falsehood those shall try,
And hard Unkindness' altered eye,
That mocks the tear it forced to flow;
And keen Remorse with blood defiled,
And moody Madness[3] laughing wild
80 Amid severest woe.

Lo, in the vale of years beneath
A grisly troop are seen,
The painful family of Death,
More hideous than their Queen:
85 This racks the joints, this fires the veins,
That every labouring sinew strains,
Those in the deeper vitals rage:
Lo, Poverty, to fill the band,
That numbs the soul with icy hand,
90 And slow-consuming Age.

3. ——Madness laughing in his ireful mood.
            Dryden's Fable of Palamon and Arcite. [II. 582].

> To each his sufferings: all are men,
> Condemned alike to groan;
> The tender for another's pain,
> The unfeeling for his own.

95   Yet ah! why should they know their fate?
> Since sorrow never comes too late,
> And happiness too swiftly flies.
> Thought would destroy their paradise.
> No more; where ignorance is bliss,

100   'Tis folly to be wise.

Sonnet [on the Death of Mr Richard West]

> In vain to me the smiling mornings shine,
> And reddening Phoebus lifts his golden fire:
> The birds in vain their amorous descant join,
> Or cheerful fields resume their green attire:

5   These ears, alas! for other notes repine,
> A different object do these eyes require.
> My lonely anguish melts no heart but mine;
> And in my breast the imperfect joys expire.
> Yet morning smiles the busy race to cheer,

10   And new-born pleasure brings to happier men:
> The fields to all their wonted tribute bear;
> To warm their little loves the birds complain.
> I fruitless mourn to him that cannot hear,
> And weep the more because I weep in vain.

Ode to Adversity

──Ζῆνα
Τὸν φϱονεῖν βϱοτοὺς ὁδώ-
σαντα, τῶ πάθει μάθαν
Θέντα κυϱίως ἔχειν.

AESCHYLUS, *in Agamemnone*

Daughter of Jove, relentless power,
Thou tamer of the human breast,
Whose iron scourge and torturing hour,
The bad affright, afflict the best!
5   Bound in thy adamantine chain
The proud are taught to taste of pain,
And purple tyrants vainly groan
With pangs unfelt before, unpitied and alone.

When first thy Sire to send on earth
10   Virtue, his darling child, designed,
To thee he gave the heavenly birth,
And bade to form her infant mind.
Stern rugged nurse! thy rigid lore
With patience many a year she bore:
15   What sorrow was, thou bad'st her know,
And from her own she learned to melt at others' woe.

Scared at thy frown terrific, fly
Self-pleasing Folly's idle brood,
Wild Laughter, Noise, and thoughtless Joy,
20   And leave us leisure to be good.
Light they disperse, and with them go
The summer friend, the flattering foe;
By vain Prosperity received,
To her they vow their truth and are again believed.

25   Wisdom in sable garb arrayed,
Immersed in rapturous thought profound,
And Melancholy, silent maid
With leaden eye, that loves the ground,

Still on thy solemn steps attend:
30   Warm Charity, the general friend,
With Justice to herself severe,
And Pity, dropping soft the sadly-pleasing tear.

Oh, gently on thy suppliant's head,
Dread goddess, lay thy chastening hand!
35   Not in thy Gorgon terrors clad,
Nor circled with the vengeful band
(As by the impious thou art seen)
With thundering voice and threatening mien,
With screaming Horror's funeral cry,
40   Despair, and fell Disease, and ghastly Poverty.

Thy form benign, oh Goddess, wear,
Thy milder influence impart,
Thy philosophic train be there
To soften, not to wound my heart,
45   The generous spark extinct revive,
Teach me to love and to forgive,
Exact my own defects to scan,
What others are, to feel, and know myself a man.

Ode on the Death of a Favourite Cat, Drowned in a Tub of Gold Fishes

'Twas on a lofty vase's side,
Where China's gayest art had dyed
        The azure flowers, that blow;
Demurest of the tabby kind,
5   The pensive Selima reclined,
        Gazed on the lake below.

Her conscious tail her joy declared;
The fair round face, the snowy beard,
    The velvet of her paws,
10 Her coat, that with the tortoise vies,
Her ears of jet, and emerald eyes,
    She saw; and purred applause.

Still had she gazed; but 'midst the tide
Two angel forms were seen to glide,
15   The genii of the stream:
Their scaly armour's Tyrian hue
Through richest purple to the view
    Betrayed a golden gleam.

The hapless nymph with wonder saw:
20 A whisker first and then a claw,
    With many an ardent wish,
She stretched in vain to reach the prize.
What female heart can gold despise?
    What cat's averse to fish?

25 Presumptuous maid! with looks intent
Again she stretched, again she bent,
    Nor knew the gulf between.
(Malignant Fate sat by, and smiled)
The slippery verge her feet beguiled,
30   She tumbled headlong in.

Eight times emerging from the flood
She mewed to every watery god,
    Some speedy aid to send.
No dolphin came, no Nereid stirred:
35 Nor cruel Tom, nor Susan heard.
    A favourite has no friend!

From hence, ye beauties, undeceived,
Know, one false step is ne'er retrieved,
    And be with caution bold.
40 Not all that tempts your wandering eyes
And heedless hearts, is lawful prize;
    Nor all that glisters gold.

Elegy Written in a Country Churchyard

The curfew tolls[1] the knell of parting day,
The lowing herd wind slowly o'er the lea,
The ploughman homeward plods his weary way,
And leaves the world to darkness and to me.

5 Now fades the glimmering landscape on the sight,
And all the air a solemn stillness holds,
Save where the beetle wheels his droning flight,
And drowsy tinklings lull the distant folds;

Save that from yonder ivy-mantled tower
10 The moping owl does to the moon complain
Of such, as wandering near her secret bower,
Molest her ancient solitary reign.

Beneath those rugged elms, that yew-tree's shade,
Where heaves the turf in many a mouldering heap,
15 Each in his narrow cell for ever laid,
The rude forefathers of the hamlet sleep.

The breezy call of incense-breathing morn,
The swallow twittering from the straw-built shed,
The cock's shrill clarion, or the echoing horn,
20 No more shall rouse them from their lowly bed.

---

1. —— squilla di lontano,
Che paia 'l giorno pianger, che si muore.
        Dante. Purgat. [*Canto*] 8. [lines 5–6].

For them no more the blazing hearth shall burn,
Or busy housewife ply her evening care:
No children run to lisp their sire's return,
Or climb his knees the envied kiss to share.

25   Oft did the harvest to their sickle yield,
Their furrow oft the stubborn glebe has broke;
How jocund did they drive their team afield!
How bowed the woods beneath their sturdy stroke!

Let not Ambition mock their useful toil,
30   Their homely joys, and destiny obscure;
Nor Grandeur hear with a disdainful smile,
The short and simple annals of the poor.

The boast of heraldry, the pomp of power,
And all that beauty, all that wealth e'er gave,
35   Awaits alike the inevitable hour.
The paths of glory lead but to the grave.

Nor you, ye proud, impute to these the fault,
If Memory o'er their tomb no trophies raise,
Where through the long-drawn aisle and fretted vault
40   The pealing anthem swells the note of praise.

Can storied urn or animated bust
Back to its mansion call the fleeting breath?
Can Honour's voice provoke the silent dust,
Or Flattery soothe the dull cold ear of Death?

45   Perhaps in this neglected spot is laid
Some heart once pregnant with celestial fire;
Hands that the rod of empire might have swayed,
Or waked to ecstasy the living lyre.

But Knowledge to their eyes her ample page
50   Rich with the spoils of time did ne'er unroll;
Chill Penury repressed their noble rage,
And froze the genial current of the soul.

Full many a gem of purest ray serene,
The dark unfathomed caves of ocean bear:
55   Full many a flower is born to blush unseen,
And waste its sweetness on the desert air.

Some village-Hampden, that with dauntless breast
The little tyrant of his fields withstood;
Some mute inglorious Milton here may rest,
60   Some Cromwell guiltless of his country's blood.

The applause of listening senates to command,
The threats of pain and ruin to despise,
To scatter plenty o'er a smiling land,
And read their history in a nation's eyes,

65   Their lot forbade: nor circumscribed alone
Their growing virtues, but their crimes confined;
Forbade to wade through slaughter to a throne,
And shut the gates of mercy on mankind,

The struggling pangs of conscious truth to hide,
70   To quench the blushes of ingenuous shame,
Or heap the shrine of Luxury and Pride
With incense kindled at the Muse's flame.

Far from the madding crowd's ignoble strife
Their sober wishes never learned to stray;
75   Along the cool sequestered vale of life
They kept the noiseless tenor of their way.

Yet even these bones from insult to protect
Some frail memorial still erected nigh,
With uncouth rhymes and shapeless sculpture decked,
80   Implores the passing tribute of a sigh.

Their name, their years, spelt by the unlettered muse,
The place of fame and elegy supply:
And many a holy text around she strews,
That teach the rustic moralist to die.

85 For who to dumb Forgetfulness a prey,
  This pleasing anxious being e'er resigned,
  Left the warm precincts of the cheerful day,
  Nor cast one longing lingering look behind?

  On some fond breast the parting soul relies,
90 Some pious drops the closing eye requires;
  Ev'n from the tomb the voice of nature cries,
  ²Ev'n in our ashes live their wonted fires.

  For thee, who mindful of the unhonoured dead,
  Dost in these lines their artless tale relate;
95 If chance, by lonely Contemplation led,
  Some kindred spirit shall inquire thy fate,

  Haply some hoary-headed swain may say,
  'Oft have we seen him at the peep of dawn
  Brushing with hasty steps the dews away
100 To meet the sun upon the upland lawn.

  'There at the foot of yonder nodding beech
  That wreathes its old fantastic roots so high,
  His listless length at noontide would he stretch,
  And pore upon the brook that babbles by.

105 'Hard by yon wood, now smiling as in scorn,
  Muttering his wayward fancies he would rove,
  Now drooping, woeful wan, like one forlorn,
  Or crazed with care, or crossed in hopeless love.

  'One morn I missed him on the customed hill,
110 Along the heath and near his favourite tree;
  Another came; nor yet beside the rill,
  Nor up the lawn, nor at the wood was he;

---

2. Ch'i veggio nel pensier, dolce mio fuoco,
Fredda una lingua, & due begli occhi chiusi
Rimaner doppo noi pien di faville.

       Petrarch. Son. 169. [actually 170].

'The next with dirges due in sad array
Slow through the church-way path we saw him borne.
115   Approach and read (for thou can'st read) the lay,
Graved on the stone beneath yon aged thorn.'

THE EPITAPH

Here rests his head upon the lap of earth
A youth to fortune and to fame unknown.
Fair Science frowned not on his humble birth,
120   *And Melancholy marked him for her own.*

Large was his bounty, and his soul sincere,
Heaven did a recompense as largely send:
He gave to Misery all he had, a tear,
He gained from Heaven ('twas all he wished) a friend.

125   *No farther seek his merits to disclose,*
Or draw his frailties from their dread abode,
(³There they alike in trembling hope repose)
The bosom of his Father and his God.

A Long Story

In Britain's isle, no matter where,
An ancient pile of building stands:
The Huntingdons and Hattons there
Employed the power of fairy hands

5   To raise the ceiling's fretted height,
Each panel in achievements clothing,
Rich windows that exclude the light,
And passages that lead to nothing.

3. ——paventosa speme.
                              Petrarch. Son. 114. [actually 115].

Full oft within the spacious walls,
10   When he had fifty winters o'er him,
My grave ¹Lord-Keeper led the brawls;
The Seal and Maces danced before him.

His bushy beard and shoe-strings green,
His high-crowned hat, and satin doublet,
15   Moved the stout heart of England's Queen,
Though Pope and Spaniard could not trouble it.

'What, in the very first beginning!
Shame of the versifying tribe!
Your history whither are you spinning?
20   Can you do nothing but describe?'

A house there is (and that's enough),
From whence one fatal morning issues
A brace of warriors, not in buff,
But rustling in their silks and tissues.

25   The first came cap-a-pee from France
Her conquering destiny fulfilling,
Whom meaner beauties eye askance,
And vainly ape her art of killing.

The other Amazon kind heaven
30   Had armed with spirit, wit, and satire:
But Cobham had the polish given,
And tipped her arrows with good-nature.

To celebrate her eyes, her air –
Coarse panegyrics would but tease her.
35   Melissa is her *nom de guerre*.
Alas, who would not wish to please her!

1. [Sir Christopher] Hatton, prefer'd by Queen Elizabeth for his graceful Person and fine Dancing.

With bonnet blue and capucine,
And aprons long they hid their armour,
And veiled their weapons bright and keen
40   In pity to the country-farmer.

Fame in the shape of Mr. P[ur]t
(By this time all the parish know it)
Had told, that thereabouts there lurked
A wicked imp they call a poet,

45   Who prowled the country far and near,
Bewitched the children of the peasants,
Dried up the cows, and lamed the deer,
And sucked the eggs, and killed the pheasants.

My lady heard their joint petition,
50   Swore by her coronet and ermine,
She'd issue out her high commission
To rid the manor of such vermin.

The heroines undertook the task,
Through lanes unknown, o'er stiles they ventured,
55   Rapped at the door, nor stayed to ask,
But bounce into the parlour entered.

The trembling family they daunt,
They flirt, they sing, they laugh, they tattle,
Rummage his mother, pinch his aunt,
60   And upstairs in a whirlwind rattle.

Each hole and cupboard they explore,
Each creek and cranny of his chamber,
Run hurry-skurry round the floor,
And o'er the bed and tester clamber,

65   Into the drawers and china pry,
Papers and books, a huge imbroglio!
Under a tea-cup he might lie,
Or creased, like dogs-ears, in a folio.

On the first marching of the troops
70   The Muses, hopeless of his pardon,
Conveyed him underneath their hoops
To a small closet in the garden.

So Rumour says (who will, believe);
But that they left the door ajar,
75   Where, safe and laughing in his sleeve,
He heard the distant din of war.

Short was his joy. He little knew,
The power of magic was no fable.
Out of the window, whisk, they flew,
80   But left a spell upon the table.

The words too eager to unriddle,
The poet felt a strange disorder:
Transparent birdlime formed the middle,
And chains invisible the border.

85   So cunning was the apparatus,
The powerful pothooks did so move him,
That, will he, nill he, to the Great-House
He went, as if the Devil drove him.

Yet on his way (no sign of grace,
90   For folks in fear are apt to pray)
To Phoebus he preferred his case,
And begged his aid that dreadful day.

The godhead would have backed his quarrel,
But with a blush on recollection
95   Owned, that his quiver and his laurel
'Gainst four such eyes were no protection.

The court was sat, the culprit there,
Forth from their gloomy mansions creeping
The Lady Janes and Joans repair,
100   And from the gallery stand peeping:

Such as in silence of the night
Come (sweep) along some winding entry
([2]Styack has often seen the sight)
Or at the chapel-door stand sentry;

105   In peaked hoods and mantles tarnished,
Sour visages, enough to scare ye,
High dames of honour once, that garnished
The drawing-room of fierce Queen Mary!

The peeress comes. The audience stare,
110   And doff their hats with due submission:
She curtsies, as she takes her chair,
To all the people of condition.

The bard with many an artful fib,
Had in imagination fenced him,
115   Disproved the arguments of [3]Squib,
And all that [4]Groom could urge against him.

But soon his rhetoric forsook him,
When he the solemn hall had seen;
A sudden fit of ague shook him,
120   He stood as mute as poor [5]Macleane.

Yet something he was heard to mutter,
'How in the park beneath an old tree
(Without design to hurt the butter,
Or any malice to the poultry),

2. The House-Keeper.

3. Groom of the Chambers.

4. The Steward.

5. A famous Highwayman hanged the week before.

125 'He once or twice had penned a sonnet;
    Yet hoped that he might save his bacon:
    Numbers would give their oaths upon it,
    He ne'er was for a conjurer taken.'

    The ghostly prudes with hagged face
130 Already had condemned the sinner.
    My lady rose and with a grace –
    She smiled, and bid him come to dinner.

    'Jesu-Maria! Madam Bridget,
    Why, what can the Viscountess mean?'
135 (Cried the square hoods in woeful fidget)
    'The times are altered quite and clean!

    'Decorum's turned to mere civility;
    Her air and all her manners show it.
    Commend me to her affability!
140 Speak to a commoner and poet!'

    (*Here 500 stanzas are lost*)

    And so God save our noble King,
    And guard us from long-winded lubbers,
    That to eternity would sing,
    And keep my lady from her rubbers.

Stanzas to Mr Bentley

    In silent gaze the tuneful choir among,
        Half pleased, half blushing, let the Muse admire,
    While Bentley leads her sister-art along,
        And bids the pencil answer to the lyre.
5   See, in their course, each transitory thought
        Fixed by his touch a lasting essence take;
    Each dream, in fancy's airy colouring wrought,
        To local symmetry and life awake!

The tardy rhymes that used to linger on,
10   To censure cold, and negligent of fame,
In swifter measures animated run,
          And catch a lustre from his genuine flame.
Ah! could they catch his strength, his easy grace,
          His quick creation, his unerring line;
15   The energy of Pope they might efface,
          And Dryden's harmony submit to mine.
But not to one in this benighted age
          Is that diviner inspiration given,
That burns in Shakespeare's or in Milton's page,
20   The pomp and prodigality of heaven.
As when, conspiring in the diamond's blaze,
          The meaner gems, that singly charm the sight,
Together dart their intermingled rays,
          And dazzle with a luxury of light.
25   Enough for me, if to some feeling breast
          My lines a secret sympathy [impart]
And as their pleasing influence [flows confessed]
          A sigh of soft reflection [heave the heart].

The Progress of Poesy. A Pindaric Ode

Φωνᾶντα συνετοῖσιν· ἐς
Δὲ τὸ πᾶν ἑρμηνέων χατίζει.

                    PINDAR, *Olymp.* II. [85]

ADVERTISEMENT

When the Author first published this and the following Ode,
he was advised, even by his Friends, to subjoin some few
explanatory Notes: but had too much respect for the under-
standing of his Readers to take that liberty.

I. 1
      [1]Awake, Aeolian lyre, awake,
And give to rapture all thy trembling strings.
From Helicon's harmonious springs
A thousand rills their mazy progress take:
5   The laughing flowers, that round them blow,
Drink life and fragrance as they flow.
Now the rich stream of music winds along,
Deep, majestic, smooth, and strong,
Through verdant vales and Ceres' golden reign:
10   Now rolling down the steep amain,
Headlong, impetuous, see it pour:
The rocks and nodding groves rebellow to the roar.

I. 2
      [2]Oh! Sovereign of the willing soul,
Parent of sweet and solemn-breathing airs,
15   Enchanting shell! the sullen Cares
And frantic Passions hear thy soft control.
On Thracia's hills the Lord of War
Has curbed the fury of his car,
And dropped his thirsty lance at thy command.
20   [3]Perching on the sceptered hand

1. Awake, my glory: awake, lute and harp.
                      David's Psalms. [57:8].
Pindar styles his own poetry with its musical accompanyments, Αἰοληῒς μολπή, Αἰολίδες χορδαί, Αἰολίδων πνοαὶ αὐλῶν, Aeolian song, Aeolian strings, the breath of the Aeolian flute.
    The subject and simile, as usual with Pindar, are united. The various sources of poetry, which gives life and lustre to all it touches, are here described; its quiet majestic progress enriching every subject (otherwise dry and barren) with a pomp of diction and luxuriant harmony of numbers; and its more rapid and irresistible course, when swoln and hurried away by the conflict of tumultuous passions.

2. Power of harmony to calm the turbulent sallies of the soul. The thoughts are borrowed from the first Pythian of Pindar [lines 5–12].

3. This is a weak imitation of some incomparable lines in the same Ode.

Of Jove, thy magic lulls the feathered king
With ruffled plumes and flagging wing:
Quenched in dark clouds of slumber lie
The terror of his beak, and lightnings of his eye.

I. 3

25   ⁴Thee the voice, the dance, obey,
Tempered to thy warbled lay.
O'er Idalia's velvet-green
The rosy-crownèd Loves are seen
On Cytherea's day
30   With antic Sports, and blue-eyed Pleasures,
Frisking light in frolic measures;
Now pursuing, now retreating,
Now in circling troops they meet:
To brisk notes in cadence beating
35   ⁵Glance their many-twinkling feet.
Slow melting strains their queen's approach declare:
Where'er she turns the Graces homage pay.
With arms sublime, that float upon the air,
In gliding state she wins her easy way:
40   O'er her warm cheek and rising bosom move
⁶The bloom of young desire and purple light of love.

II. 1

          ⁷Man's feeble race what ills await,
Labour, and penury, the racks of pain,
Disease, and sorrow's weeping train,
45   And death, sad refuge from the storms of fate!

4. Power of harmony to produce all the graces of motion in the body.

5. Μαρμαρυγὰς θηεῖτο ποδῶν, θαύμαζε δὲ θυμῷ.
                                HOMER. Od. Θ. [VIII. 265].

6. Λάμπει δ' ἐπὶ πορφυρέῃσι
Παρείῃσι φῶς ἔρωτος.
          PHRYNICHUS, apud Athenaeum. [Deipnosophistae, XIII. 604a].

7. To compensate the real and imaginary ills of life, the Muse was given to
Mankind by the same Providence that sends the Day by its chearful presence
to dispel the gloom and terrors of the Night.

The fond complaint, my song, disprove,
And justify the laws of Jove.
Say, has he given in vain the heavenly Muse?
Night, and all her sickly dews,
50   Her spectres wan, and birds of boding cry,
He gives to range the dreary sky:
⁸Till down the eastern cliffs afar
Hyperion's march they spy, and glittering shafts of war.

II. 2
       ⁹In climes beyond the solar¹⁰ road,
55   Where shaggy forms o'er ice-built mountains roam,
The Muse has broke the twilight-gloom
To cheer the shivering native's dull abode.
And oft, beneath the odorous shade
Of Chile's boundless forests laid,
60   She deigns to hear the savage youth repeat
In loose numbers wildly sweet
Their feather-cinctured chiefs, and dusky loves.
Her track, where'er the goddess roves,
Glory pursue, and generous Shame,
65   The unconquerable Mind, and Freedom's holy flame.

8. Or seen the Morning's well-appointed Star
Come marching up the eastern hills afar.
                    Cowley [*Brutus, an ode*, stanza IV, lines 58–9].

9. Extensive influence of poetic Genius over the remotest and most uncivilized
nations: its connection with liberty, and the virtues that naturally attend on it.
(See the Erse, Norwegian, and Welch Fragments, the Lapland and American
songs.)

10. 'Extra anni solisque vias——'
                    Virgil [*Aeneid*, VI. 796].
'Tutta lontana dal camin del sole.'
                    Petrarch, Canzon 2. [line 48].

II. 3

[11]"Woods that wave o'er Delphi's steep,
Isles that crown the Aegean deep,
Fields that cool Ilissus laves,
Or where Maeander's amber waves
70 In lingering lab'rinths creep,
How do your tuneful echoes languish,
Mute, but to the voice of anguish?
Where each old poetic mountain
Inspiration breathed around:
75 Every shade and hallowed fountain
Murmured deep a solemn sound:
Till the sad Nine in Greece's evil hour
Left their Parnassus for the Latian plains.
Alike they scorn the pomp of tyrant-power,
80 And coward Vice that revels in her chains.
When Latium had her lofty spirit lost,
They sought, oh Albion! next thy sea-encircled coast.

III. 1

Far from the sun and summer-gale,
In thy green lap was [12]Nature's darling laid,
85 What time, where lucid Avon strayed,
To him the mighty Mother did unveil
Her awful face: the dauntless child
Stretched forth his little arms and smiled.
'This pencil take,' (she said) 'whose colours clear
90 Richly paint the vernal year:
Thine too these golden keys, immortal boy!
This can unlock the gates of joy;
Of horror that, and thrilling fears,
Or ope the sacred source of sympathetic tears.'

11. Progress of Poetry from Greece to Italy, and from Italy to England.
Chaucer was not unacquainted with the writings of Dante or of Petrarch.
The Earl of Surrey and Sir Tho. Wyatt had travelled in Italy, and formed
their taste there; Spenser imitated the Italian writers; Milton improved on
them: but this School expired soon after the Restoration, and a new one
arose on the French model, which has subsisted ever since.

12. Shakespear.

III. 2

95   Nor second he,[13] that rode sublime
Upon the seraph-wings of Ecstasy,
The secrets of the abyss to spy.
[14]He passed the flaming bounds of place and time:
[15]The living throne, the sapphire-blaze,
100   Where angels tremble while they gaze,
He saw; but blasted with excess of light,
[16]Closed his eyes in endless night.
Behold, where Dryden's less presumptuous car,
Wide o'er the fields of glory bear
105   [17]Two coursers of ethereal race,
[18]With necks in thunder clothed, and long-resounding pace.

III. 3

Hark, his hands the lyre explore!
Bright-eyed Fancy hovering o'er
Scatters from her pictured urn
110   [19]Thoughts that breathe, and words that burn.

13. Milton.

14. '——flammantia moenia mundi.'
                    Lucretius [*De Rerum Natura*, I. 73].

15. For the spirit of the living creature was in the wheels – And above the
firmament, that was over their heads, was the likeness of a throne, as
the appearance of a saphire-stone. – This was the appearance of the glory of
the Lord.
         Ezekiel 1:20, 26, 28.

16. Ὀφθαλμῶν μὲν ἄμερσε· δίδου δ' ἡδεῖαν ἀοιδήν.
                    HOMER. Od. [VIII. 64].

17. Meant to express the stately march and sounding energy of Dryden's
rhimes.

18. Hast thou cloathed his neck with thunder?
                    Job [39:19].

19. Words, that weep, and tears that speak.
                    Cowley [*The Prophet*, line 20].

²⁰But ah! 'tis heard no more –
Oh! lyre divine, what daring spirit
Wakes thee now? Though he inherit
Nor the pride, nor ample pinion,
115   ²¹That the Theban eagle bear
Sailing with supreme dominion
Through the azure deep of air:
Yet oft before his infant eyes would run
Such forms, as glitter in the Muse's ray
120   With orient hues, unborrowed of the sun:
Yet shall he mount, and keep his distant way
Beyond the limits of a vulgar fate,
Beneath the Good how far – but far above the Great.

The Bard. A Pindaric Ode

ADVERTISEMENT

The following Ode is founded on a Tradition current in Wales,
that Edward the First, when he compleated the Conquest of
that country, ordered all the Bards, that fell into his hands,
to be put to death.

---

20. We have had in our language no other odes of the sublime kind, than
that of Dryden on St. Cecilia's day: for Cowley (who had his merit) yet
wanted judgment, style, and harmony, for such a task. That of Pope is not
worthy of so great a man. Mr. Mason indeed of late days has touched the
true chords, and with a masterly hand, in some of his Choruses, – above all
in the last of Caractacus,
Hark! heard ye not yon footstep dread? &c.

21. Διὸς πρὸς ὄρνιχα θεῖον.
Olymp. 2 [line 88]. Pindar compares himself to that bird, and his enemies
to ravens that croak and clamour in vain below, while it pursues its flight,
regardless of their noise.

I. 1

    'Ruin seize thee, ruthless king!
Confusion on thy banners wait,
Though fanned by Conquest's crimson wing
[1]They mock the air with idle state.
5 Helm nor [2]hauberk's twisted mail,
Nor even thy virtues, tyrant, shall avail
To save thy secret soul from nightly fears,
From Cambria's curse, from Cambria's tears!'
Such were the sounds, that o'er the [3]crested pride
10 Of the first Edward scattered wild dismay,
As down the steep of [4]Snowdon's shaggy side
He wound with toilsome march his long array.
Stout [5]Gloucester stood aghast in speechless trance:
'To arms!' cried [6]Mortimer, and couched his quivering
     lance.

1. Mocking the air with colours idly spread.
                       Shakespear's King John [V. i. 72].

2. The Hauberk was a texture of steel ringlets, or rings interwoven, form-
ing a coat of mail, that sate close to the body, and adapted itself to every
motion.

3. —— The crested adder's pride.
                       Dryden's Indian Queen [perhaps III. i,
                       but there is no precise correspondence].

4. *Snowdon* was a name given by the Saxons to that mountainous tract, which
the Welch themselves call *Craigian-eryri*: it included all the highlands of
Caernarvonshire and Merionethshire, as far east as the river Conway.
R. Hygden speaking of the castle of Conway built by King Edward the first,
says, 'Ad ortum amnis Conway ad clivum montis Erery'; and Matthew of
Westminster, (ad ann. 1283,) 'Apud Aberconway ad pedes montis Snowdoniae
fecit erigi castrum forte.'

5. Gilbert de Clare, surnamed the Red, Earl of Gloucester and Hertford,
son-in-law to King Edward.

6. Edmond de Mortimer, Lord of Wigmore.
  They both were *Lords-Marchers*, whose lands lay on the borders of Wales,
and probably accompanied the King in this expedition.

I. 2

15   On a rock, whose haughty brow
Frowns o'er old Conway's foaming flood,
Robed in the sable garb of woe,
With haggard eyes the poet stood;
([7]Loose his beard, and hoary hair
20   [8]Streamed, like a meteor, to the troubled air)
And with a master's hand, and prophet's fire,
Struck the deep sorrows of his lyre.
'Hark, how each giant-oak, and desert cave
Sighs to the torrent's awful voice beneath!
25   O'er thee, oh king! their hundred arms they wave,
Revenge on thee in hoarser murmurs breathe;
Vocal no more, since Cambria's fatal day,
To high-born Hoël's harp, or soft Llewellyn's lay.

I. 3

      'Cold is Cadwallo's tongue,
30   That hushed the stormy main:
Brave Urien sleeps upon his craggy bed:
Mountains, ye mourn in vain
Modred, whose magic song
Made huge Plinlimmon bow his cloud-topped head.
35   [9]On dreary Arvon's shore they lie,
Smeared with gore, and ghastly pale:
Far, far aloof the affrighted ravens sail;
The famished [10]eagle screams, and passes by.

7. The image was taken from a well-known picture of Raphael, representing the Supreme Being in the vision of Ezekiel: there are two of these paintings (both believed original), one at Florence, the other at Paris.

8. Shone, like a meteor, streaming to the wind.
Milton's Paradise Lost [I. 537].

9. The shores of Caernarvonshire opposite to the isle of Anglesey.

10. Cambden and others observe, that eagles used annually to build their aerie among the rocks of Snowdon, which from thence (as some think) were named by the Welch *Craigian-eryri*, or the crags of the eagles. At this day (I am told) the highest point of Snowdon is called *the eagle's nest*. That bird is certainly no stranger to this island, as the Scots, and the people of Cumberland,

Dear lost companions of my tuneful art,
40   [11]Dear, as the light that visits these sad eyes,
[11]Dear, as the ruddy drops that warm my heart,
Ye died amidst your dying country's cries –
No more I weep. They do not sleep.
On yonder cliffs, a grisly band,
45   I see them sit, they linger yet,
Avengers of their native land:
With me in dreadful harmony [12]they join,
And [12]weave with bloody hands the tissue of thy line.'

II. I
     'Weave the warp, and weave the woof,
50   The winding-sheet of Edward's race.
Give ample room, and verge enough
The characters of hell to trace.
Mark the year and mark the night,
[13]When Severn shall re-echo with affright
55   The shrieks of death, through Berkeley's roofs that ring,
Shrieks of an agonising king!
[14]She-wolf of France, with unrelenting fangs,
That tear'st the bowels of thy mangled mate,
[15]From thee be born, who o'er thy country hangs
60   The scourge of heaven. What terrors round him wait!
Amazement in his van, with Flight combined,
And Sorrow's faded form, and Solitude behind.

Westmoreland, &c. can testify; it even has built its nest in the Peak of Derbyshire. (See Willoughby's Ornithol. published by Ray.)

11. As dear to me as are the ruddy drops,
That visit my sad heart——
                    Shakesp. Jul. Caesar [II. i. 289–90].

12. See the Norwegian Ode, that follows [*The Fatal Sisters*].

13. Edward the Second, cruelly butchered in Berkley-Castle [in 1327].

14. Isabel of France, Edward the Second's adulterous Queen.

15. Triumphs of Edward the Third in France.

II. 2

   'Mighty victor, mighty lord,
[16]Low on his funeral couch he lies!
65 No pitying heart, no eye, afford
 A tear to grace his obsequies.
 Is the sable [17]warrior fled?
 Thy son is gone. He rests among the dead.
 The swarm that in thy noon-tide beam were born?
70 Gone to salute the rising morn.
 Fair[18] laughs the morn and soft the zephyr blows,
 While proudly riding o'er the azure realm
 In gallant trim the gilded vessel goes;
 Youth on the prow, and Pleasure at the helm;
75 Regardless of the sweeping whirlwind's sway,
 That, hushed in grim repose, expects his evening-prey.

II. 3

   [19]'Fill high the sparkling bowl,
 The rich repast prepare,
 Reft of a crown, he yet may share the feast:
80 Close by the regal chair
 Fell Thirst and Famine scowl
 A baleful smile upon their baffled guest.
 Heard ye the din of [20]battle bray,
 Lance to lance, and horse to horse?
85 Long years of havoc urge their destined course,
 And through the kindred squadrons mow their way.

16. Death of that King, abandoned by his Children, and even robbed in his last moments by his Courtiers and his Mistress [in 1377].

17. Edward, the Black Prince, dead some time before his Father [in 1376].

18. Magnificence of Richard the Second's reign. See Froissard, and other contemporary Writers.

19. Richard the Second, (as we are told by Archbishop Scroop and the confederate Lords in their manifesto, by Thomas of Walsingham, and all the older Writers,) was starved to death [in 1400]. The story of his assassination by Sir Piers of Exon, is of much later date.

20. Ruinous civil wars of York and Lancaster.

Ye towers of Julius[21], London's lasting shame,
With many a foul and midnight murther fed,
Revere his [22]consort's faith, his father's [23]fame,
90   And spare the meek [24]usurper's holy head.
Above, below, the [25]rose of snow,
Twined with her blushing foe, we spread:
The bristled [26]Boar in infant-gore
Wallows beneath thy thorny shade.
95   Now, brothers, bending o'er the accursed loom,
Stamp we our vengeance deep, and ratify his doom.

III. 1

        'Edward, lo! to sudden fate
(Weave we the woof. The thread is spun)
[27]Half of thy heart we consecrate.
100   (The web is wove. The work is done.)'
'Stay, oh stay! nor thus forlorn
Leave me unblessed, unpitied, here to mourn:
In yon bright track, that fires the western skies,
They melt, they vanish from my eyes.

21. Henry the Sixth, George Duke of Clarence, Edward the Fifth, Richard Duke of York, &c. believed to be murthered secretly in the Tower of London. The oldest part of that structure is vulgarly attributed to Julius Caesar.

22. Margaret of Anjou, a woman of heroic spirit, who struggled hard to save her Husband and her Crown.

23. Henry the Fifth.

24. Henry the Sixth very near being canonized. The line of Lancaster had no right of inheritance to the Crown.

25. The white and red roses, devices of York and Lancaster.

26. The silver Boar was the badge of Richard the Third; whence he was usually known in his own time by the name of *the Boar*.

27. Eleanor of Castile died [in 1290] a few years after the conquest of Wales. The heroic proof she gave of her affection for her Lord is well known. The monuments of his regret, and sorrow for the loss of her, are still to be seen at Northampton, Geddington, Waltham, and other places.

105 But oh! what solemn scenes on Snowdon's height
     Descending slow their glittering skirts unroll?
     Visions of glory, spare my aching sight,
     Ye unborn ages, crowd not on my soul!
     No more our long-lost [28]Arthur we bewail.
110 All-hail, [29]ye genuine kings, Britannia's issue, hail!

III. 2
          'Girt with many a baron bold
     Sublime their starry fronts they rear;
     And gorgeous dames, and statesmen old
     In bearded majesty, appear.
115 In the midst a form divine!
     Her eye proclaims her of the Briton-line;
     Her lion-port[30], her awe-commanding face,
     Attempered sweet to virgin-grace.
     What strings symphonious tremble in the air,
120 What strains of vocal transport round her play!
     Hear from the grave, great Taliessin[31], hear;
     They breathe a soul to animate thy clay.
     Bright Rapture calls, and soaring, as she sings,
     Waves in the eye of heaven her many-coloured wings.

28. It was the common belief of the Welch nation, that King Arthur was still alive in Fairy-Land, and should return again to reign over Britain.

29. Both Merlin and Taliessin had prophesied, that the Welch should regain their sovereignty over this island; which seemed to be accomplished in the House of Tudor.

30. Speed relating an audience given by Queen Elizabeth to Paul Dzialinski, Ambassadour of Poland, says, 'And thus she, lion-like rising, daunted the malapert Orator no less with her stately port and majestical deporture, than with the tartnesse of her princelie checkes.'

31. Taliessin, Chief of the Bards, flourished in the VIth Century. His works are still preserved, and his memory held in high veneration among his Countrymen.

III. 3

125   'The verse adorn again
        [32]Fierce war and faithful love,
        And truth severe, by fairy fiction dressed.
        In [33]buskined measures move
        Pale Grief, and pleasing Pain,
130   With Horror, tyrant of the throbbing breast.
        A [34]voice, as of the cherub-choir,
        Gales from blooming Eden bear;
        [35]And distant warblings lessen on my ear,
        That lost in long futurity expire.
135   Fond impious man, think'st thou, yon sanguine cloud,
        Raised by thy breath, has quenched the orb of day?
        Tomorrow he repairs the golden flood,
        And warms the nations with redoubled ray.
        Enough for me: with joy I see
140   The different doom our fates assign.
        Be thine despair and sceptered care;
        To triumph, and to die, are mine.'
        He spoke, and headlong from the mountain's height
        Deep in the roaring tide he plunged to endless night.

The Fatal Sisters. An Ode

ADVERTISEMENT

The Author once had thoughts (in concert with a Friend) of giving *the History of English Poetry*: In the Introduction to it he meant to have produced some specimens of the Style that

---

32. Fierce wars and faithful loves shall moralize my song.
                    Spenser's Proëme to the Fairy Queen [I. 9].

33. Shakespear.

34. Milton.

35. The succession of Poets after Milton's time.

reigned in ancient times among the neighbouring nations, or those who had subdued the greater part of this Island, and were our Progenitors: the following three Imitations made a part of them. He has long since drop'd his design, especially after he had heard, that it was already in the hands of a Person well qualified to do it justice, both by his taste, and his researches into antiquity.

PREFACE

In the Eleventh Century *Sigurd*, Earl of the Orkney-Islands, went with a fleet of ships and a considerable body of troops into Ireland, to the assistance of *Sictryg with the silken beard*, who was then making war on his father-in-law *Brian*, King of Dublin: the Earl and all his forces were cut to pieces, and *Sictryg* was in danger of a total defeat; but the enemy had a greater loss by the death of *Brian*, their King, who fell in the action. On Christmas-day, (the day of the battle,) a Native of *Caithness* in Scotland saw at a distance a number of persons on horseback riding full speed towards a hill, and seeming to enter into it. Curiosity led him to follow them, till looking through an opening in the rocks he saw twelve gigantic figures resembling women: they were all employed about a loom; and as they wove, they sung the following dreadful Song; which when they had finished, they tore the web into twelve pieces, and (each taking her portion) galloped Six to the North and as many to the South.

Note – The *Valkyriur* were female Divinities, Servants of *Odin* (or *Woden*) in the Gothic mythology. Their name signifies *Chusers of the slain*. They were mounted on swift horses, with drawn swords in their hands; and in the throng of battle selected such as were destined to slaughter, and conducted them to *Valhalla*, the hall of *Odin*, or paradise of the Brave; where they attended the banquet, and served the departed Heroes with horns of mead and ale.

Now the storm begins to lower,
(Haste, the loom of hell prepare,)
[1]Iron-sleet of arrowy shower
[2]Hurtles in the darkened air.

5   Glittering lances are the loom,
Where the dusky warp we strain,
Weaving many a soldier's doom,
Orkney's woe, and Randver's bane.

See the grisly texture grow,
10   ('Tis of human entrails made,)
And the weights that play below,
Each a gasping warrior's head.

Shafts for shuttles, dipped in gore,
Shoot the trembling cords along.
15   Sword, that once a monarch bore,
Keep the tissue close and strong.

Mista black, terrific maid,
Sangrida and Hilda see,
Join the wayward work to aid:
20   'Tis the woof of victory.

E're the ruddy sun be set,
Pikes must shiver, javelins sing,
Blade with clattering buckler meet,
Hauberk crash and helmet ring.

25   (Weave the crimson web of war)
Let us go, and let us fly,
Where our friends the conflict share,
Where they triumph, where they die.

1. How quick they wheel'd; and flying, behind them shot
Sharp sleet of arrowy shower——
                    Milton's Par. Regained [III. 323–4].

2. The noise of battle hurtled in the air.
                    Shakesp. Jul. Caesar [II. ii. 22].

As the paths of fate we tread,
30 Wading through the ensanguined field:
Gondula and Geira, spread
O'er the youthful king your shield.

We the reins to slaughter give,
Ours to kill and ours to spare:
35 Spite of danger he shall live.
(Weave the crimson web of war.)

They, whom once the desert-beach
Pent within its bleak domain,
Soon their ample sway shall stretch
40 O'er the plenty of the plain.

Low the dauntless earl is laid,
Gored with many a gaping wound:
Fate demands a nobler head;
Soon a king shall bite the ground.

45 Long his loss shall Eirin weep,
Ne'er again his likeness see;
Long her strains in sorrow steep,
Strains of immortality!

Horror covers all the heath,
50 Clouds of carnage blot the sun.
Sisters, weave the web of death;
Sisters, cease, the work is done.

Hail the task, and hail the hands!
Songs of joy and triumph sing!
55 Joy to the victorious bands;
Triumph to the younger king.

Mortal, thou that hear'st the tale,
Learn the tenor of our song.
Scotland, through each winding vale
60 Far and wide the notes prolong.

Sisters, hence with spurs of speed:
Each her thundering faulchion wield;
Each bestride her sable steed.
Hurry, hurry to the field.

[*The Death of Hoël*]

Had I but the torrent's might,
With headlong rage and wild affright
Upon Deïra's squadrons hurled,
To rush, and sweep them from the world!
5   Too, too secure in youthful pride,
By them my friend, my Hoël, died,
Great Cian's son: of Madoc old
He asked no heaps of hoarded gold;
Alone in nature's wealth arrayed,
10 He asked, and had the lovely maid.
      To Cattraeth's vale in glittering row
Twice two hundred warriors go;
Every warrior's manly neck
Chains of regal honour deck,
15 Wreathed in many a golden link:
From the golden cup they drink
Nectar, that the bees produce,
Or the grape's ecstatic juice.
Flushed with mirth and hope they burn:
20 But none from Cattraeth's vale return,
Save Aëron brave, and Conan strong,
(Bursting through the bloody throng)
And I, the meanest of them all,
That live to weep and sing their fall.

[*Sketch of His Own Character*]

Too poor for a bribe, and too proud to importune;
He had not the method of making a fortune:
Could love, and could hate, so was thought somewhat odd;
No very great wit, he believed in a God.
5   A post or a pension he did not desire,
But left church and state to Charles Townshend and Squire.

The Candidate

When sly Jemmy Twitcher had smugged up his face
With a lick of court whitewash, and pious grimace,
A-wooing he went, where three sisters of old
In harmless society guttle and scold.
5   'Lord! Sister,' says Physic to Law, 'I declare
Such a sheep-biting look, such a pick-pocket air,
Not I, for the Indies! you know I'm no prude;
But his nose is a shame, and his eyes are so lewd!
Then he shambles and straddles so oddly, I fear –
10   No; at our time of life, 'twould be silly, my dear.'
        'I don't know,' says Law, 'now methinks, for his look,
'Tis just like the picture in Rochester's book.
But his character, Phyzzy, his morals, his life;
When she died, I can't tell, but he once had a wife.
15   'They say he's no Christian, loves drinking and whoring,
And all the town rings of his swearing and roaring,
His lying, and filching, and Newgate-bird tricks:–
Not I, – for a coronet, chariot and six.'
        Divinity heard, between waking and dozing,
20   Her sisters denying, and Jemmy proposing;
From dinner she rose with her bumper in hand,
She stroked up her belly and stroked down her band.
        'What a pother is here about wenching and roaring!
Why, David loved catches and Solomon whoring.

25   Did not Israel filch from the Egyptians of old
     Their jewels of silver and jewels of gold?
     The prophet of Bethel, we read, told a lie;
     He drinks: so did Noah; he swears: so do I.
     To refuse him for such peccadilloes, were odd;
30   Besides, he repents, and he talks about G[od].
          'Never hang down your head, you poor penitent elf!
     Come, buss me, I'll be Mrs Twitcher myself.
     D[am]n ye both for a couple of Puritan bitches!
     He's Christian enough that repents and that [stitches].'

On L[or]d H[olland']s Seat near M[argat]e, K[en]t

     Old and abandoned by each venal friend,
          Here H[olland] took the pious resolution
     To smuggle some few years and strive to mend
          A broken character and constitution.
5   On this congenial spot he fixed his choice;
          Earl Godwin trembled for his neighbouring sand:
     Here sea-gulls scream and cormorants rejoice,
          And mariners, though shipwrecked, dread to land.
     Here reign the blustering North and blighting East,
10   No tree is heard to whisper, bird to sing:
     Yet nature cannot furnish out the feast,
          Art he invokes new horrors still to bring.
     Now mouldering fanes and battlements arise,
          Arches and turrets nodding to their fall,
15   Unpeopled palaces delude his eyes,
          And mimic desolation covers all.
     'Ah', said the sighing peer, 'had Bute been true,
          Nor Shelburne's, Rigby's, Calcraft's friendship vain,
     Far other scenes than these had blessed our view
20   And realised the ruins that we feign.
     Purged by the sword and beautified by fire,
          Then had we seen proud London's hated walls:
     Owls might have hooted in St Peter's choir,
          And foxes stunk and littered in St Paul's.'

CHARLES CHURCHILL

Poems

A NOTE ON THE TEXT

Churchill's poems generally present few textual problems. Most of them first appeared individually in quarto pamphlets. They were later collected into two quarto volumes, one in 1763, the text of which is unreliable, and one in 1765, after Churchill's death, which is more reliable, and which incorporates some changes made by Churchill for the purpose of this re-publication.

Copy text for this edition is that of the first edition, unless the poem was subsequently altered by Churchill, in which case the last edition to be so altered is used. Copy text for 'The Crab', recently unearthed by Lance Bertelson and added to the Churchill canon, derives from Churchill's letter to Wilkes in the British Library.

For the full text of Churchill's poems in its original eighteenth-century appearance, the reader should consult Douglas Grant's edition of *The Poetical Works of Charles Churchill* (Oxford, 1956).

The Apology. Addressed to the Critical Reviewers

> Tristitiam et metus
> Tradam protervis in mare *criticum*
> Portare ventis

Laughs not the heart when giants, big with pride,
Assume the pompous port, the martial stride;
O'er arm Herculean heave the enormous shield,
Vast as a weaver's beam the javelin wield;
5   With the loud voice of thundering Jove defy,
And dare to single combat – What? – A fly.

And laugh we less when giant names, which shine
Established as it were by right divine;
Critics whom every captive art adores,
10 To whom glad Science pours forth all her stores;
Who high in lettered reputation sit,
And hold, Astraea-like, the scales of Wit;
With partial rage rush forth – Oh! shame to tell! –
To crush a bard just bursting from the shell?

15 Great are his perils in this stormy time
Who rashly ventures on a sea of rhyme.
Around vast surges roll, winds envious blow,
And jealous rocks and quicksands lurk below.
Greatly his foes he dreads, but more his friends;
20 He hurts me most who lavishly commends.

Look through the world – in every other trade
The same employment's cause of kindness made;
At least appearance of good will creates;
And every fool puffs off the fool he hates:
25 Cobblers with cobblers smoke away the night,
And in the common cause e'en players unite.
Authors alone, with more than savage rage,
Unnatural war with brother authors wage.

The pride of nature would as soon admit
30   Competitors in empire as in wit.
Onward they rush at Fame's imperious call,
And, less than greatest, would not be at all.

Smit with the love of honour – or the pence,
O'er-run with wit, and destitute of sense,
35   If any novice in the rhyming trade,
With lawless pen the realms of verse invade;
Forth from the court, where sceptered sages sit,
Abused with praise, and flattered into wit;
Where in lethargic majesty they reign,
40   And what they won by dullness still maintain;
Legions of factious authors throng at once;
Fool beckons fool, and dunce awakens dunce.
To H[a]m[i]lt[o]n's the ready lies repair –
Ne'er was lie made which was not welcome there.
45   Thence, on maturer judgement's anvil wrought,
The polished falsehood's into public brought.
Quick circulating slanders mirth afford,
And reputation bleeds in every word.

A Critic was of old a glorious name,
50   Whose sanction handed merit up to fame:
Beauties as well as faults he brought to view:
His judgment great, and great his candour too.
No servile rules drew sickly taste aside;
Secure he walked, for Nature was his guide.
55   But now, oh strange reverse! our critics bawl
In praise of candour with a heart of gall.
Conscious of guilt, and fearful of the light,
They lurk enshrouded in the veil of night:
Safe from detection, seize the unwary prey,
60   And stab, like bravoes, all who come that way.

When first my Muse, perhaps more bold than wise,
Bade the rude trifle into light arise,
Little she thought such tempests would ensue,
Less, that those tempests would be raised by you.

65   The thunder's fury rends the towering oak,
     Rosciads, like shrubs, might 'scape the fatal stroke.
     Vain thought! A critic's fury knows no bound;
     Drawcansir like, he deals destruction round;
     Nor can we hope he will a stranger spare
70   Who gives no quarter to his friend Voltaire.

       Unhappy genius! placed, by partial Fate,
     With a free spirit in a slavish state;
     Where the reluctant Muse, oppressed by kings,
     Or droops in silence, or in fetters sings.
75   In vain thy dauntless fortitude hath borne
     The bigot's furious zeal, and tyrant's scorn.
     Why did'st thou safe from home-bred dangers steer?
     Reserved to perish more ignobly here.
     Thus, when the Julian tyrant's pride to swell
80   Rome with her Pompey at Pharsalia fell,
     The vanquished chief escaped from Caesar's hand
     To die by ruffians in a foreign land.

       How could these self-elected monarchs raise
     So large an empire on so small a base?
85   In what retreat, inglorious and unknown,
     Did Genius sleep when Dullness seized the throne?
     Whence, absolute now grown, and free from awe,
     She to the subject world dispenses law.
     Without her licence, not a letter stirs;
90   And all the captive criss cross row is hers.
     The Stagyrite, who rules from Nature drew,
     Opinions gave, but gave his reasons too.
     Our great dictators take a shorter way –
     Who shall dispute what the Reviewers say?
95   Their word's sufficient; and to ask a reason,
     In such a state as theirs, is downright treason.
     True judgment, now, with them alone can dwell;
     Like church of Rome they're grown infallible.
     Dull superstitious readers they deceive,
100 Who pin their easy faith on critic's sleeve,
     And, knowing nothing, every thing believe!

But why repine we, that these puny elves
Shoot into giants? – We may thank ourselves.
Fools that we are, like Israel's fools of yore,
105 The calf ourselves have fashioned we adore.
But let true Reason once resume her reign,
This god shall dwindle to a calf again.

Founded on arts which shun the face of day,
By the same arts they still maintain their sway.
110 Wrapped in mysterious secrecy they rise,
And, as they are unknown, are safe and wise.
At whomsoever aimed, howe'er severe
The envenomed slander flies, no names appear.
Prudence forbid that step. – Then all might know,
115 And on more equal terms engage the foe.
But now, what Quixote of the age would care
To wage a war with dirt, and fight with air?
By interest joined, the expert confederates stand,
And play the game into each other's hand.
120 The vile abuse, in turn by all denied,
Is bandied up and down from side to side:
It flies – hey presto! like a juggler's ball,
Till it belongs to nobody at all.

All men and things they know, themselves unknown,
125 And publish every name – except their own.
Nor think this strange – secure from vulgar eyes
The nameless author passes in disguise.
But veteran critics are not so deceived,
If veteran critics are to be believed.
130 Once seen they know an author evermore,
Nay, swear to hands they never saw before.
Thus in the *Rosciad*, beyond chance or doubt,
They, by the writing, found the writers out.
'That's Lloyd's – his manner there you plainly trace,
135 And all the *Actor* stares you in the face.
By Colman that was written. – On my life,
The strongest symptoms of the *Jealous Wife*.

That little disingenuous piece of spite,
Churchill, a wretch unknown, perhaps might write.'
140　How doth it make judicious readers smile,
When authors are detected by their style:
Though every one who knows this author, knows
He shifts his style much oftener than his clothes?

Whence could arise this mighty critic spleen,
145　The Muse a trifler, and her theme so mean?
What had I done, that angry Heaven should send
The bitterest foe, where most I wished a friend?
Oft hath my tongue been wanton at thy name,
And hailed the honours of thy matchless fame.
150　For me let hoary Fielding bite the ground
So nobler Pickle stand superbly bound.
From Livy's temples tear the historic crown
Which with more justice blooms upon thine own.
Compared with thee, be all life-writers dumb,
155　But he who wrote the Life of Tommy Thumb.
Who ever read the *Regicide* but swore
The author wrote as man ne'er wrote before?
Others for plots and under-plots may call,
Here's the right method – have no plot at all.
160　Who can so often in his cause engage
The tiny pathos of the Grecian stage,
Whilst horrors rise, and tears spontaneous flow
At tragic Ha! and no less tragic Oh!?
His nervous weakness all to praise agree;
165　And then, for sweetness, who so sweet as he?
Too big for utterance when sorrows swell
The too big sorrows flowing tears must tell:
But when those flowing tears shall cease to flow,
Why, – then the voice must speak again you know.

170　Rude and unskilful in the poet's trade,
I kept no naiads by me ready-made;
Ne'er did I colours high in air advance,
Torn from the bleeding fopperies of France:

No flimsey linsey-woolsey scenes I wrote
175   With patches here and there like Joseph's coat.
Me humbler themes befit. Secure, for me,
Let playwrights smuggle nonsense duty free:
Secure, for me, ye lambs, ye lambkins bound,
And frisk and frolic o'er the fairy ground:
180   Secure, for me, thou pretty little faun
Lick Sylvia's hand, and crop the flowery lawn:
Uncensured let the gentle breezes rove,
Through the green umbrage of the enchanted grove:
Secure, for me, let foppish Nature smile,
185   And play the coxcomb in the *Desert Isle*.

The stage I chose – a subject fair and free –
'Tis yours – 'tis mine – 'tis public property.
All common exhibitions open lie
For praise or censure to the common eye.
190   Hence are a thousand hackney-writers fed;
Hence Monthly Critics earn their daily bread.
This is a general tax which all must pay,
From those who scribble, down to those who play.
Actors, a venal crew, receive support
195   From public bounty, for the public sport.
To clap or hiss, all have an equal claim,
The cobbler's and his lordship's right the same.
All join for their subsistence; all expect
Free leave to praise their worth, their faults correct.
200   When active Pickle Smithfield stage ascends,
The three days wonder of his laughing friends;
Each, or as judgement, or as fancy guides,
The lively witling praises or derides.
And where's the mighty difference, tell me where,
205   Betwixt a Merry Andrew and a player?

The strolling tribe, a despicable race,
Like wandering Arabs, shift from place to place.
Vagrants by law, to justice open laid,
They tremble, of the beadle's lash afraid,

210 And fawning cringe, for wretched means of life,
    To Madam Mayoress or his Worship's Wife.

        The mighty monarch, in theatric sack,
    Carries his whole regalia at his back;
    His royal consort heads the female band,
215 And leads the heir-apparent in her hand;
    The panniered ass creeps on with conscious pride,
    Bearing a future prince on either side.
    No choice musicians in this troop are found
    To varnish nonsense with the charms of sound;
220 No swords, no daggers, not one poisoned bowl;
    No lightning flashes here, no thunders roll;
    No guards to swell the monarch's train are shown;
    The monarch here must be an host alone.
    No solemn pomp, no slow processions here;
225 No Ammon's entry and no Juliet's bier.

        By need compelled to prostitute his art,
    The varied actor flies from part to part;
    And, strange disgrace to all theatric pride,
    His character is shifted with his side.
230 Question and Answer he by turns must be,
    Like that small wit in modern tragedy;
    Who, to support his fame, – or fill his purse, –
    Still pilfers wretched plans, and makes them worse;
    Like gipsies, lest the stolen brat be known,
235 Defacing first, then claiming for his own.
    In shabby state they strut, and tattered robe;
    The scene a blanket, and a barn the globe.
    No high conceits their moderate wishes raise,
    Content with humble profit, humble praise.
240 Let dowdies simper, and let bumpkins stare,
    The strolling pageant hero treads in air:
    Pleased for his hour he to mankind gives law,
    And snores the next out on a truss of straw.

        But if kind Fortune, who we sometimes know
245 Can take a hero from a puppet-show,

In mood propitious should her favourite call,
On royal stage in royal pomp to bawl,
Forgetful of himself he rears the head,
And scorns the dunghill where he first was bred:
250   Conversing now with well-dressed kings and queens,
With gods and goddesses behind the scenes,
He sweats beneath the terror-nodding plume,
Taught by mock honours real pride to assume.
On this great stage the world, no monarch e'er
255   Was half so haughty as a monarch-player.

Doth it more move our anger or our mirth
To see these *things*, the lowest sons of earth,
Presume, with self-sufficient knowledge graced,
To rule in letters and preside in taste?
260   The town's decisions they no more admit,
Themselves alone the arbiters of wit;
And scorn the jurisdiction of that court
To which they owe their being and support.
Actors, like monks of old, now sacred grown,
265   Must be attacked by no fools but their own.

Let the vain tyrant sit amidst his guards,
His puny greenroom wits and venal bards,
Who meanly tremble at the puppet's frown,
And for a playhouse freedom lose their own;
270   In spite of new-made laws, and new-made kings,
The free-born Muse with liberal spirit sings,
Bow down, ye slaves; before these idols fall;
Let Genius stoop to them who've none at all;
Ne'er will I flatter, cringe, or bend the knee
275   To those who, slaves to all, are slaves to me.

Actors, as actors, are a lawful game;
The poet's right; and who shall bar his claim?
And, if o'er-weening of their little skill,
When they have left the stage they're actors still;
280   If to the subject world they still give laws,
With paper crowns, and sceptres made of straws;

If they in cellar or in garret roar,
And kings one night, are kings for evermore;
Shall not bold Truth, e'en there, pursue her theme,
285   And wake the coxcomb from his golden dream?
Or if, well worthy of a better fate,
They rise superior to their present state;
If, with each social virtue graced, they blend
The gay companion and the faithful friend;
290   If they, like Pritchard, join in private life
The tender parent and the virtuous wife;
Shall not our verse their praise with pleasure speak,
Though mimics bark and envy split her cheek?
No honest worth's beneath the Muse's praise;
295   No greatness can above her censure raise:
Station and wealth, to her, are trifling things;
She stoops to actors, and she soars to kings.

Is there a man, in vice and folly bred,
To sense of honour as to virtue dead;
300   Whom ties nor human, nor divine, can bind;
Alien to God, and foe to all mankind;
Who spares no character; whose every word,
Bitter as gall, and sharper than the sword,
Cuts to the quick; whose thoughts with rancour swell:
305   Whose tongue, on earth, performs the work of Hell?
If there be such a monster, the *Reviews*
Shall find him holding forth against abuse.
'Attack Profession! – 'tis a deadly breach!
The Christian laws another lesson teach:
310   Unto the end should charity endure,
And Candour hide those faults it cannot cure.'
Thus Candour's maxims flow from Rancour's throat,
As devils, to serve their purpose, scripture quote.

The Muse's office was by Heaven designed,
315   To please, improve, instruct, reform mankind;
To make dejected Virtue nobly rise
Above the towering pitch of splendid Vice;

To make pale Vice, abashed, her head hang down,
And trembling crouch at Virtue's awful frown.
320   Now armed with wrath, she bids eternal shame,
With strictest justice, brand the villain's name:
Now in the milder garb of Ridicule
She sports, and pleases while she wounds the fool.
Her shape is often varied; but her aim,
325   To prop the cause of Virtue, still the same.
In praise of Mercy let the guilty bawl,
When Vice and Folly for correction call;
Silence the mark of weakness justly bears,
And is partaker of the crimes it spares.

330   But if the Muse, too cruel in her mirth,
With harsh reflections wound the man of worth;
If wantonly she deviate from her plan,
And quits the actor to expose the man;
Ashamed, she marks that passage with a blot,
335   And hates the line where Candour was forgot.

But what is Candour, what is Humour's vein,
Though Judgement join to consecrate the strain,
If curious numbers will not aid afford,
Nor choicest music play in every word?
340   Verses must run, to charm a modern ear,
From all harsh, rugged interruptions clear:
Soft let them breathe, as Zephyr's balmy breeze;
Smooth let their current flow as summer seas;
Perfect then only deemed when they dispense
345   A happy tuneful vacancy of sense.
Italian fathers thus, with barbarous rage,
Fit helpless infants for the squeaking stage;
Deaf to the calls of pity, Nature wound,
And mangle vigour for the sake of sound.
350   Henceforth farewell then, feverish thirst of fame;
Farewell the longings for a poet's name;
Perish my Muse; – a wish 'bove all severe
To him who ever held the Muses dear,

If e'er her labours weaken to refine
355   The generous roughness of a nervous line.

Others affect the stiff and swelling phrase;
Their Muse must walk in stilts and strut in stays:
The sense they murder, and the words transpose,
Lest poetry approach too near to prose.
360   See, tortured Reason, how they pare and trim,
And, like Procrustes, stretch or lop the limb.

Waller, whose praise succeeding bards rehearse,
Parent of harmony in English verse,
Whose tuneful Muse in sweetest accent flows,
365   In couplets first taught straggling sense to close.

In polished numbers, and majestic sound,
Where shall thy rival, Pope, be ever found?
But whilst each line with equal beauty flows,
E'en excellence, unvaried, tedious grows.
370   Nature, through all her works, in great degree,
Borrows a blessing from variety.
Music itself her needful aid requires
To rouse the soul, and wake our dying fires.
Still in one key, the nightingale would tease:
375   Still in one key, not Brent would always please.

Here let me bend, great Dryden, at thy shrine,
Thou dearest name to all the tuneful nine.
What if some dull lines in cold order creep,
And with his theme the poet seems to sleep?
380   Still when his subject rises proud to view,
With equal strength the poet rises too.
With strong invention, noblest vigour fraught,
Thought still springs up and rises out of thought;
Numbers, ennobling numbers in their course,
385   In varied sweetness flow, in varied force;
The powers of Genius and of Judgement join,
And the whole art of poetry is thine.

But what are numbers, what are bards to me,
Forbid to tread the paths of poesy?
390 'A sacred muse should consecrate her pen;
Priests must not hear nor see like other men;
Far higher themes should her ambition claim;
Behold where Sternhold points the way to Fame.'

Whilst, with mistaken zeal, dull bigots burn,
395 Let Reason for a moment take her turn.
When coffee-sages hold discourse with kings,
And blindly walk in paper leading-strings,
What if a man delight to pass his time
In spinning Reason into harmless rhyme;
400 Or sometimes boldly venture to the play?
Say, where's the crime? – great man of prudence, say?
No two on earth in one thing can agree,
All have some darling singularity.
Women and men, as well as girls and boys,
405 In gew-gaws take delight, and sigh for toys.
Your sceptres, and your crowns, and such like things,
Are but a better kind of toys for kings.
In things indifferent, Reason bids us choose,
Whether the whim's a monkey or a Muse.

410 What the grave triflers on this busy scene,
When they make use of this word Reason, mean,
I know not; but, according to my plan,
'Tis Lord-Chief-Justice in the Court of Man,
Equally formed to rule in age and youth,
415 The friend of virtue and the guide to truth.
To her I bow, whose sacred power I feel;
To her decision make my last appeal;
Condemned by her, applauding worlds in vain
Should tempt me to resume the pen again:
420 By her absolved, my course I'll still pursue:
If Reason's for me, God is for me too.

The Conference

Grace said in form, which sceptics must agree,
When they are told that grace was said by me;
The servants gone, to break the scurvy jest
On the proud landlord, and his thread-bare guest;
5   The King gone round, my Lady too withdrawn,
My Lord, in usual taste, began to yawn,
And lolling backward in his elbow-chair,
With an insipid kind of stupid stare,
Picking his teeth, twirling his seals about –
10   'Churchill, You have a poem coming out.
You've my best wishes; but I really fear
Your Muse in general is too severe,
Her spirit seems her interest to oppose,
And where she makes one friend, makes twenty foes.'

15   C. 'Your Lordship's fears are just, I feel their force,
But only feel it as a thing of course.
The man, whose hardy spirit shall engage
To lash the vices of a guilty age,
At his first setting forward ought to know,
20   That every rogue he meets must be his foe,
That the rude breath of Satire will provoke
Many who feel, and more who fear the stroke.
But shall the partial rage of selfish men
From stubborn Justice wrench the righteous pen,
25   Or shall I not my settled course pursue,
Because my foes, are foes to Virtue too?'

        L. 'What is this boasted Virtue, taught in schools,
And idly drawn from antiquated rules?
What is her use? point out one wholesome end?
30   Will she hurt foes, or can she make a friend?
When from long fasts fierce appetites arise,
Can this same Virtue stifle Nature's cries?
Can she the pittance of a meal afford,
Or bid thee welcome to one great man's board?

35 When northern winds the rough December arm
With frost and snow, can Virtue keep thee warm?
Canst thou dismiss the hard unfeeling dun
Barely by saying, thou art Virtue's son?
Or by base blundering statesmen sent to jail,
40 Will Mansfield take this Virtue for thy bail?
Believe it not, the name is in disgrace,
Virtue and Temple now are out of place.

'Quit then this meteor, whose delusive ray
From wealth and honour leads thee far astray.
45 True Virtue means, let Reason use her eyes,
Nothing with fools, and interest with the wise.
Would'st thou be great, her patronage disclaim,
Nor madly triumph in so mean a name:
Let nobler wreaths thy happy brows adorn,
50 And leave to Virtue poverty and scorn.
Let Prudence be thy guide: who doth not know
How seldom Prudence can with Virtue go?
To be successful try thy utmost force,
And Virtue follows as a thing of course.

55 'Hirco, who knows not Hirco, stains the bed
Of that kind master who first gave him bread,
Scatters the seeds of discord through the land,
Breaks every public, every private band,
Beholds with joy a trusting friend undone,
60 Betrays a brother, and would cheat a son:
What mortal in his senses can endure
The name of Hirco, for the wretch is poor?
"Let him hang, drown, starve, on a dunghill rot,
By all detested live, and die forgot;
65 Let him, a poor return, in every breath
Feel all death's pains, yet be whole years in death,"
Is now the general cry we all pursue;
Let Fortune change, and Prudence changes too,
Supple and pliant a new system feels,
70 Throws up her cap, and spaniels at his heels,

Long live great Hirco, cries, by interest taught,
And let his foes, though I prove one, be nought.'

    C. 'Peace to such men, if such men can have peace,
Let their possessions, let their state increase,
75 Let their base services in courts strike root,
And in the season bring forth golden fruit,
I envy not; let those who have the will,
And, with so little spirit, so much skill
With such vile instruments their fortunes carve;
80 Rogues may grow fat, an honest man dares starve.'

    L. 'These stale conceits thrown off, let us advance
For once to real life, and quit Romance.
Starve! pretty talking! but I fain would view
That man, that honest man would do it too.
85 Hence to yon mountain which outbraves the sky,
And dart from pole to pole thy strengthened eye,
Through all that space you shall not view one man,
Not one, who dares to act on such a plan.
Cowards in calms will say, what in a storm
90 The brave will tremble at, and not perform.
Thine be the proof, and, spite of all you've said,
You'd give your honour for a crust of bread.'

    C. 'What Proof might do, what Hunger might effect,
What famished Nature, looking with neglect
95 On all she once held dear, what Fear, at strife
With fainting Virtue for the means of life,
Might make this coward flesh, in love with breath,
Shuddering at pain, and shrinking back from death,
In treason to my soul, descend to bear,
100 Trusting to Fate, I neither know, nor care.

    'Once, at this hour those wounds afresh I feel,
Which nor Prosperity nor Time can heal,
Those wounds, which Fate severely hath decreed,
Mentioned or thought of, must for ever bleed,

105 Those wounds, which humbled all that pride of man,
Which brings such mighty aid to Virtue's plan;
Once, awed by Fortune's most oppressive frown,
By legal rapine to the earth bowed down,
My credit at last gasp, my state undone,
110 Trembling to meet the shock I could not shun,
Virtue gave ground, and blank despair prevailed;
Sinking beneath the storm, my spirits failed,
Like Peter's faith, till one, a friend indeed,
May all distress find such in time of need,
115 One kind good man, in act, in word, in thought,
By Virtue guided, and by Wisdom taught,
Image of him whom Christians should adore,
Stretched forth his hand, and brought me safe to shore.

'Since, by good fortune into notice raised,
120 And for some little merit largely praised,
Indulged in swerving from prudential rules,
Hated by rogues, and not beloved by fools,
Placed above want, shall abject thirst of wealth
So fiercely war 'gainst my soul's dearest health,
125 That, as a boon, I should base shackles crave,
And, born to Freedom, make myself a slave;
That I should in the train of those appear,
Whom Honour cannot love, nor manhood fear?

'That I no longer skulk from street to street,
130 Afraid lest duns assail, and bailiffs meet;
That I from place to place this carcase bear,
Walk forth at large, and wander free as air;
That I no longer dread the awkward friend,
Whose very obligations must offend,
135 Nor, all too froward, with impatience burn
At suffering favours which I can't return;
That, from dependence and from pride secure,
I am not placed so high to scorn the poor,
Nor yet so low, that I my Lord should fear,
140 Or hesitate to give him sneer for sneer;

That, whilst sage Prudence my pursuits confirms,
I can enjoy the world on equal terms;
That, kind to others, to myself most true,
Feeling no want, I comfort those who do,
145   And with the will have power to aid distress;
These, and what other blessings I possess,
From the indulgence of the Public rise;
All private patronage my soul defies.
By candour more inclined to save, than damn,
150   A generous Public made me what I am.
All that I have, they gave; just memory bears
The grateful stamp, and what I am is theirs.'

  L. 'To feign a red-hot zeal for freedom's cause,
To mouth aloud for liberties and laws,
155   For Public good to bellow all abroad,
Serves well the purposes of private fraud.
Prudence, by Public good intends her own;
If you mean otherwise, you stand alone.
What do we mean by Country and by Court,
160   What is it to oppose, what to support?
Mere words of course, and what is more absurd
Than to pay homage to an empty word!
Majors and minors differ but in name,
Patriots and Ministers are much the same;
165   The only difference, after all their rout,
Is that the one is *in*, the other *out*.

  'Explore the dark recesses of the mind,
In the soul's honest volume read mankind,
And own, in wise and simple, great and small,
170   The same grand leading principle in all.
Whate'er we talk of wisdom to the wise,
Of goodness to the good, of public ties
Which to our country link, of private bands
Which claim most dear attention at our hands,
175   For parent and for child, for wife and friend,
Our first great mover, and our last great end,

Is one, and by whatever name we call
The ruling tyrant, Self is all in all.
This, which unwilling Faction shall admit,
180   Guided in different ways a Bute and Pitt,
Made tyrants break, made kings observe the law,
And gave the world a Stuart and Nassau.

'Hath Nature (strange and wild conceit of Pride)
Distinguished thee from all her sons beside?
185   Doth Virtue in thy bosom brighter glow,
Or from a spring more pure doth action flow?
Is not thy soul bound with those very chains
Which shackle us, or is that Self, which reigns
O'er kings and beggars, which in all we see
190   Most strong and sovereign, only weak in thee?
Fond man, believe it not; experience tells
'Tis not thy virtue, but thy pride rebels.
Think, and for once lay by thy lawless pen;
Think, and confess thyself like other men;
195   Think but one hour, and, to thy conscience led
By Reason's hand, bow down and hang thy head;
Think on thy private life, recall thy youth,
View thyself now, and own with strictest truth,
That Self hath drawn thee from fair Virtue's way
200   Farther than Folly would have dared to stray,
And that the talents liberal Nature gave
To make thee free, have made thee more a slave.

'Quit then, in prudence quit, that idle train
Of toys, which have so long abused thy brain,
205   And captive led thy powers; with boundless will
Let Self maintain her state and empire still,
But let her, with more worthy objects caught,
Strain all the faculties and force of thought
To things of higher daring; let her range
210   Through better pastures, and learn how to change;
Let her, no longer to weak Faction tied,
Wisely revolt, and join our stronger side.'

  C. 'Ah! what, my Lord, hath private life to do
With things of public nature? why to view
215 Would you thus cruelly those scenes unfold,
Which, without pain and horror to behold,
Must speak me something more, or less than man;
Which friends may pardon, but I never can?
Look back! a thought which borders on despair,
220 Which human nature must, yet cannot bear.
'Tis not the babbling of a busy world,
Where praise and censure are at random hurled,
Which can the meanest of my thoughts control,
Or shake one settled purpose of my soul.
225 Free and at large might their wild curses roam,
If all, if all alas! were well at home.
No – 'tis the tale which angry Conscience tells,
When she with more than tragic horror swells
Each circumstance of guilt; when stern, but true,
230 She brings bad actions forth into review;
And, like the dread hand-writing on the wall,
Bids late Remorse awake at Reason's call,
Armed at all points bids scorpion Vengeance pass,
And to the mind holds up Reflection's glass,
235 The mind, which starting, heaves the heart-felt groan,
And hates that form she knows to be her own.

  'Enough of this – let private sorrows rest –
As to the Public I dare stand the test;
Dare proudly boast, I feel no wish above
240 The good of England, and my country's love.
Stranger to Party-rage, by Reason's voice,
Unerring guide, directed in my choice,
Not all the tyrant powers of earth combined,
No, nor of hell, shall make me change my mind.
245 What! herd with men my honest soul disdains,
Men who, with servile zeal, are forging chains
For Freedom's neck, and lend a helping hand,
To spread destruction o'er my native land.
What! shall I not, e'en to my latest breath,
250 In the full face of danger and of death,

Exert that little strength which Nature gave,
And boldly stem, or perish in the wave?'

    L. 'When I look backward for some fifty years,
And see protesting Patriots turn'd to peers;
255 Hear men, most loose, for decency declaim,
And talk of character, without a name;
See infidels assert the cause of God,
And meek divines wield persecution's rod;
See men transformed to brutes, and brutes to men,
260 See Whitehead take a place, Ralph change his pen,
I mock the zeal, and deem the men in sport,
Who rail at Ministers, and curse a Court.
Thee, haughty as thou art, and proud in rhyme,
Shall some preferment, offered at a time
265 When Virtue sleeps, some sacrifice to Pride,
Or some fair victim, move to change thy side.
Thee shall these eyes behold, to health restored,
Using, as Prudence bids, bold Satire's sword,
Galling thy present friends, and praising those,
270 Whom now thy frenzy holds thy greatest foes.'

    C. 'May I (can worse disgrace on manhood fall?)
Be born a Whitehead, and baptised a Paul;
May I (though to his service deeply tied
By sacred oaths, and now by will allied)
275 With false feigned zeal an injured God defend,
And use his name for some base private end;
May I (that thought bids double horrors roll
O'er my sick spirits, and unmans my soul)
Ruin the Virtue which I held most dear,
280 And still must hold; may I, through abject fear,
Betray my friend; may to succeeding times,
Engraved on plates of adamant, my crimes
Stand blazing forth, whilst marked with envious blot,
Each little act of Virtue is forgot;
285 Of all those evils which, to stamp men cursed,
Hell keeps in store for vengeance, may the worst

Light on my head, and in my day of woe,
To make the cup of bitterness o'erflow,
May I be scorned by every man of worth,
290   Wander, like Cain, a vagabond on earth,
Bearing about a hell in my own mind,
Or be to Scotland for my life confined,
If I am one amongst the many known,
Whom Shelburne fled, and Calcraft blushed to own.'

295   *L.* 'Do you reflect what men you make your foes?'

       C. 'I do, and that's the reason I oppose.
Friends I have made, whom Envy must commend,
But not one foe, whom I would wish a friend.
What if ten thousand Butes and Foxes bawl,
300   One Wilkes hath made a large amends for all.

       'Tis not the title, whether handed down
From age to age, or flowing from the crown
In copious streams on recent men, who came
From stems unknown, and sires without a name;
305   'Tis not the Star, which our great Edward gave
To mark the virtuous, and reward the brave,
Blazing without, whilst a base heart within
Is rotten to the core with filth and sin;
'Tis not the tinsel grandeur, taught to wait,
310   At custom's call, to mark a fool of State
From fools of lesser note, that soul can awe
Whose pride is Reason, whose defence is Law.'

       L. 'Suppose (a thing scarce possible in Art,
Were it thy cue to play a common part;)
315   Suppose thy writings so well fenced in Law,
That N[orton] cannot find, nor make a flaw,
Hast thou not heard, that 'mongst our ancient tribes
By Party warped, or lulled asleep by bribes,
Or trembling at the ruffian hand of Force,
320   Law hath suspended stood, or changed its course?

Art thou assured, that, for destruction ripe,
Thou mayst not smart beneath the self-same gripe?
What sanction hast thou, frantic in thy rhymes,
Thy life, thy freedom to secure?'

                                     C. 'The times.

325 'Tis not on Law, a system great and good,
By Wisdom penned, and bought by noblest blood,
My faith relies: by wicked men and vain,
Law, once abused, may be abused again. –
No, on our great Law-giver I depend,
330 Who knows and guides her to her proper end;
Whose royalty of nature blazes out
So fierce, 'twere sin to entertain a doubt –
Did tyrant Stuarts now the laws dispense
(Blessed be the hour and hand which sent them hence)
335 For something, or for nothing, for a word,
Or thought, I might be doomed to death, unheard.
Life we might all resign to lawless Power,
Nor think it worth the purchase of an hour;
But Envy ne'er shall fix so foul a stain
340 On the fair annals of a Brunswick's reign.

    'If, slave to Party, to Revenge, or Pride,
If, by frail human error drawn aside,
I break the Law, strict rigour let her wear;
'Tis hers to punish, and 'tis mine to bear,
345 Nor, by the voice of Justice doomed to death,
Would I ask mercy with my latest breath.
But, anxious only for my country's good,
In which my King's, of course, is understood;
Formed on a plan with some few Patriot friends,
350 Whilst by just means I aim at noblest ends,
My spirits cannot sink; though from the tomb
Stern Jeffreys should be placed in Mansfield's room,
Though he should bring, his base designs to aid,
Some black attorney, for his purpose made,
355 And shove, whilst Decency and Law retreat,
The modest Norton from his maiden seat,

Though both, in ill confederates, should agree,
In damned league, to torture Law and Me,
Whilst George is king, I cannot fear endure;
360   Not to be guilty, is to be secure.

'But when in after-times (be far removed
That day) our monarch, glorious and beloved,
Sleeps with his fathers, should imperious Fate
In vengeance with fresh Stuarts curse our state;
365   Should they, o'erleaping every fence of Law,
Butcher the brave to keep tame fools in awe;
Should they, by brutal and oppressive force,
Divert sweet Justice from her even course;
Should they, of every other means bereft,
370   Make my right hand a witness 'gainst my left;
Should they, abroad by inquisitions taught,
Search out my soul, and damn me for a thought,
Still would I keep my course, still speak, still write,
Till Death had plunged me in the shades of Night.

375   'Thou God of Truth, thou great, all-searching eye,
To whom our thoughts, our spirits open lie,
Grant me thy strength, and in that needful hour,
(Should it e'er come) when Law submits to Power,
With firm resolves my steady bosom steel,
380   Bravely to suffer, though I deeply feel.

'Let me, as hitherto, still draw my breath,
In love with life, but not in fear of death,
And, if Oppression brings me to the grave,
And marks me dead, she ne'er shall mark a slave.
385   Let no unworthy marks of grief be heard,
No wild laments, not one unseemly word;
Let sober triumphs wait upon my bier,
I won't forgive that friend who drops one tear.
Whether he's ravished in life's early morn,
390   Or, in old age, drops like an ear of corn,
Full ripe he falls, on Nature's noblest plan,
Who lives to Reason, and who dies a man.'

The Crab

– Tibi brachia contrahit ardens
  Cancer –

Whoever studies humankind
Devoid of prejudice, will find,
       Whatever priests pretend,
That they like us are flesh and blood,
5   And were before, and since the flood,
       And will be to the end.

This truth since all the learned own,
Without excepting pious Stone,
       E'en let the bigots rail;
10   Their rage but shows them in the wrong,
Then, not to make my prelude long,
       Why here begins my tale.

A priest of more than Irish fame,
Tradition says, but hides his name,
15   Who in his younger days,
Instead of mumbling over beads,
Had done in love surprising deeds,
       And cropped immortal bays,

Began to find at fifty five
20   That though each member seemed alive,
       And each in vigour still,
Yet one would often droop its head,
And spite of what he did or said,
       Refuse to work his will.

25   A sad discovery you'll say
For one who in the month of May
       Had fixed upon a night

To meet an healthy buxom bride
Whose wants a husband ill supplied,
30   And yet who knew her right.

Not go was to proclaim his case,
But then to suffer a disgrace! –
     'Ne'er fright yourself, good Sir',
Said Doctor Ward, 'when Nature halts,
35 Experience shows us certain Salts
     Will set her on the spur;

'This doctrine Cleopatra knew,
And thence luxuriously drew
     Ecstatic draughts of pleasure;
40 Crabs, cockles, when the Queen was lewd
The Roman's appetite renewed
     And Oysters were a treasure.'

In May the inhabitants of cloisters
Are too well fed to look for oysters;
45   Aye true, but crabs are plenty;
So quick to Billingsgate he goes
And of the largest picked and chose
     And sent the lady twenty.

So many crabs the wondering wife
50 Had never seen in all her life;
     Quick to her room she fled,
And not to leave them in the way,
For fear of what the world might say,
     Hid them beneath the bed.

55 There long they lay in silent state
Till one impatient of his fate,
     Or urged by Lord knows what,
Crawled out with many an awkward stride,
And waiting the return of tide
60   Stole in a neighbouring pot.

The rest they stewed with spice and wine
In proper time, and broiled the chine,
    I'd swear no grace was said;
He gave no respite to his jaws,
65 By his advice she sucked the claws,
    Then hurried up to bed.

While he was fumbling at his hose,
Madam was whipped between the clothes,
    And squat on that machine
70 (In vain we talk of style or mode)
From whence the royal favours flowed
    Of great Pomonqué Queen,

And where the crab lay snug and still
Who having quickly drank his fill
75   Would eat as well as drink,
And fearless of the rattling shower
Stretched forth a claw with all his power
    And seized the mossy brink.

What stubborn Amazonian heart
80 But must have failed at such a smart,
In such a tender spot;
'Mercy!', she shrieking cried, dismayed,
'O Man of God! quick lend your aid,
    There's death within the pot.'

85 The priest to her assistance flew,
Pulled up her shift in haste to view
    From whence those cries arose;
And whilst he mused on what he saw
The pendant Crab stretched the other claw
90   And caught him by the nose.

'God's wounds!', he cried (for priests will swear),
Then groaned as if his end was near,
    Like Florimel in labour;

The dame too now with fresh surprise
95 Redoubled quick her treble cries
And frightened every neighbour.

Both pulled and tugged with might and main,
Used every art, but all in vain,
    To heighten their disaster;
100 The more they pulled, the more they cried,
The wicked crab with cruel pride
    Still gripped and clung the faster.

Now all the street was in a clatter,
All wondering what could be the matter,
105   Half dressed ran aunts and cousins;
Some one thing, some another swore,
Howe'er, at length they burst the door
    And tumbled in by dozens.

And now while all supposed a rape,
110 Or murder in some dreadful shape,
    And every cheek grew pale;
Imagine how at once they grinned
To see the prelate's nostrils pinned
    So close to madam's tail.

115 Imagine their surprise to hear
Some oaths which not a Turk would swear,
    With now and then an 'Ave';
While madam, wriggling to and fro,
Now laboured to dislodge the foe,
120   Now tired, cried 'peccavi'.

Consider too the husband's face
To find a crab in such a place
    So curiously suspended;
And then conceive – but what a jest,
125 Without my aid you'll guess the rest,
    And so my story's ended.

'Your story ended! prithee, friend,
This never sure can be the end
    In spite of what you say;
130 You stop because your spirits fail,
Now Durfey would have told this tale
    In quite a different way.

'We want to know the prelate's shame
And of the crab too what became,
135   And can't compound for less.
But you in strange pretended haste
For want of wit bid men of taste
    Conceive, imagine, guess.'

What moral then would you infer?
140 'A tale should have a moral, sir';
    A moral! thus it flows:
On him misfortunes still attend,
Who in the secrets of a friend
    Imprudent thrusts his nose.

The Times

The time hath been, a boyish, blushing time,
When modesty was scarcely held a crime,
When the most wicked had some touch of grace,
And trembled to meet Virtue face to face,
5 When those, who, in the cause of Sin grown grey,
Had served her without grudging day by day,
Were yet so weak an awkward shame to feel,
And strove that glorious service to conceal;
We, better bred, and than our sires more wise,
10 Such paltry narrowness of soul despise,
To Virtue every mean pretence disclaim,
Lay bare our crimes, and glory in our shame.

Time was, e're Temperance had fled the realm;
E're Luxury sat guttling at the helm
15 From meal to meal, without one moment's space
Reserved for business, or allowed for grace;
E're Vanity had so far conquered Sense
To make us all wild rivals in expense,
To make one fool strive to outvie another,
20 And every coxcomb dress against his brother;
E're banished Industry had left our shores,
And Labour was by Pride kicked out of doors;E're Idleness
prevailed sole queen in courts,
Or only yielded to a rage for sports;
25 E're each weak mind was with externals caught,
And Dissipation held the place of Thought;
E're gambling Lords in Vice so far were gone
To cog the die, and bid the sun look on;
E're a great nation, not less just than free,
30 Was made a beggar by Economy;
E're rugged Honesty was out of vogue,
E're Fashion stamped her sanction on the rogue;
Time was, that men had conscience, that they made
Scruples to owe, what never could be paid.

35 Was one then found, however high his name,
So far above his fellows damned to shame,
Who dared abuse, and falsify his trust,
Who, being great, yet dared to be unjust,
Shunned like a plague, or but at distance viewed,
40 He walked the crowded streets in solitude,
Nor could his rank, and station in the land
Bribe one mean knave to take him by the hand.
Such rigid maxims (Oh, might such revive
To keep expiring Honesty alive)
45 Made rogues, all other hopes of fame denied,
Not just through principle, be just through pride.

Our times, more polished, wear a different face;
Debts are an honour; payment a disgrace.

Men of weak minds, high-placed on Folly's list,
50   May gravely tell us trade cannot subsist,
Nor all those thousands who're in trade employed,
If faith 'twixt man and man is once destroyed.
Why – be it so – we in that point accord,
But what is trade, and tradesmen, to a Lord?

55   Faber, from day to day, from year to year,
Hath had the cries of tradesmen in his ear,
Of tradesmen by his villainy betrayed,
And, vainly seeking justice, bankrupts made.
What is't to Faber? Lordly as before,
60   He sits at ease, and lives to ruin more.
Fixed at his door, as motionless as stone,
Begging, but only begging for their own,
Unheard they stand, or only heard by those,
Those slaves in livery, who mock their woes.
65   What is't to Faber? he continues great,
Lives on in grandeur, and runs out in state.
The helpless widow, wrung with deep despair,
In bitterness of soul, pours forth her prayer,
Hugging her starving babes, with streaming eyes,
70   And calls down vengeance, vengeance from the skies.
What is't to Faber? he stands safe and clear,
Heaven can commence no legal action here,
And on his breast a mighty plate he wears,
A plate more firm than triple brass, which bears
75   The name of Privilege, 'gainst vulgar awe;
He feels no conscience, and he fears no law.

Nor think, acquainted with small knaves alone,
Who have not shame outlived, and grace outgrown,
The great world hidden from thy reptile view,
80   That on such men, to whom contempt is due,
Contempt shall fall, and their vile author's name
Recorded stand through all the land of shame.
No – to his porch, like Persians to the sun,
Behold contending crowds of courtiers run;

85   See, to his aid what noble troops advance,
      All sworn to keep his crimes in countenance.
      Nor wonder at it – they partake the charge,
      As small their conscience, and their debts as large.

         Propped by such clients, and without control
90   From all that's honest in the human soul,
      In grandeur mean, with insolence unjust,
      Whilst none but knaves can praise, and fools will trust,
      Caressed and courted, Faber seems to stand
      A mighty pillar in a guilty land.
95   And (a sad truth to which succeeding times
      Will scarce give credit, when 'tis told in rhymes)
      Did not strict Honour with a jealous eye
      Watch round the throne, did not true Piety
      (Who, linked with Honour for the noblest ends,
100   Ranks none but honest men amongst her friends)
      Forbid us to be crushed with such a weight,
      He might in time be Minister of State.

         But why enlarge I on such petty crimes?
      They might have shocked the faith of former times,
105   But now are held as nothing – we begin,
      Where our sires ended, and improve in sin,
      Rack our invention, and leave nothing new
      In vice and folly for our sons to do.

         Nor deem this censure hard; there's not a place
110   Most consecrate to purposes of grace,
      Which Vice hath not polluted; none so high,
      But with bold pinion she hath dared to fly,
      And build there for her pleasure; none so low,
      But she hath crept into it, made it know,
115   And feel her power; in courts, in camps she reigns,
      O'er sober citizens, and simple swains,
      E'en in our temples she hath fixed her throne,
      And 'bove God's holy altars placed her own.

More to increase the horror of our state,
120   To make her empire lasting as 'tis great,
To make us in full-grown perfection feel
Curses which neither art nor time can heal,
All shame discarded, all remains of pride,
Meanness sits crowned, and triumphs by her side.
125   Meanness, who gleans out of the human mind
Those few good seeds which Vice had left behind,
Those seeds which might in time to Virtue tend,
And leaves the Soul without a power to mend;
Meanness, at sight of whom, with brave disdain
130   The breast of manhood swells, but swells in vain,
Before whom honour makes a forced retreat,
And Freedom is compelled to quit her seat;
Meanness which, like that mark by bloody Cain
Borne in his forehead for a brother slain,
135   God, in his great and all-subduing rage,
Ordains the standing mark of this vile age.

The venal hero trucks his fame for gold,
The Patriot's virtue for a place is sold,
The statesman bargains for his country's shame,
140   And for preferment priests their God disclaim.
Worn out with lust, her day of lechery o'er,
The mother trains the daughter which she bore
In her own paths; the father aids the plan,
And, when the innocent is ripe for man,
145   Sells her to some old lecher for a wife,
And makes her an adulteress for life,
Or in the papers bids his name appear,
And advertises for a L[igonier];
Husband and wife (whom Avarice must applaud)
150   Agree to save the charge of pimp and bawd;
Those parts they play themselves, a frugal pair,
And share the infamy, the gain to share,
Well-pleased to find, when they the profits tell,
That they have played the whore and rogue so well.

155   Nor are these things (which might imply a spark
         Of shame still left) transacted in the dark.
         No – to the public they are open laid,
         And carried on like any other trade.
         Scorning to mince damnation, and too proud
160   To work the works of darkness in a cloud,
         In fullest vigour Vice maintains her sway:
         Free are her marts, and open at noon-day.
         Meanness, now wed to Impudence, no more
         In darkness skulks, and trembles as of yore
165   When the light breaks upon her coward eye;
         Boldly she stalks on earth, and to the sky
         Lifts her proud head, nor fears lest time abate,
         And turn her husband's love to cankered hate,
         Since Fate, to make them more sincerely one,
170   Hath crowned their loves with Montagu their son.
         A son, so like his dam, so like his sire,
         With all the mother's craft, the father's fire,
         An image so express in every part,
         So like in all bad qualities of heart,
175   That, had they fifty children, he alone
         Would stand as heir apparent to the throne.

         With our own island vices not content,
         We rob our neighbours on the continent,
         Dance Europe round, and visit every court
180   To ape their follies, and their crimes import.
         To different lands for different sins we roam,
         And, richly freighted, bring our cargo home,
         Nobly industrious to make vice appear
         In her full state, and perfect only here.

185   To Holland, where Politeness ever reigns,
         Where primitive Sincerity remains,
         And makes a stand, where Freedom in her course
         Hath left her name, though she hath lost her force
         In that, as other lands, where simple trade
190   Was never in the garb of fraud arrayed,

Where Avarice never dared to show his head,
Where, like a smiling cherub, Mercy, led
By Reason, blesses the sweet-blooded race,
And Cruelty could never find a place,
195   To Holland for that Charity we roam,
Which happily begins, and ends at home.

France, in return for peace and power restored,
For all those countries, which the hero's sword
Unprofitably purchased, idly thrown
200   Into her lap, and made once more her own,
France hath afforded large and rich supplies
Of vanities full-trimmed, of polished lies,
Of soothing flatteries, which through the ears
Steal to, and melt the heart, of slavish fears
205   Which break the spirit, and of abject fraud –
For which alas! we need not send abroad.

Spain gives us Pride – which Spain to all the earth
May largely give, nor fear herself a dearth –
Gives us that Jealousy, which, born of fear
210   And mean distrust, grows not by Nature here –
Gives us that Superstition, which pretends
By the worst means to serve the best of ends –
That Cruelty, which, stranger to the brave,
Dwells only with the coward, and the slave,
215   That Cruelty, which led her Christian bands
With more than savage rage o'er savage lands,
Bade her without remorse whole countries thin,
And hold of nought, but Mercy, as a sin.

Italia, nurse of every softer art,
220   Who, feigning to refine, unmans the heart,
Who lays the realms of Sense and Virtue waste,
Who mars whilst she pretends to mend our taste,
Italia, to complete and crown our shame,
Sends us a fiend, and Legion is his name.
225   The farce of greatness, without being great,
Pride without power, titles without estate,

Souls without vigour, bodies without force,
Hate without cause, revenge without remorse,
Dark, mean revenge, murder without defence,
230 Jealousy without love, sound without sense,
Mirth without humour, without wit grimace,
Faith without reason, gospel without grace,
Zeal without knowledge, without nature art,
Men without manhood, women without heart,
235 Half-men, who, dry and pithless, are debarred
From man's best joys – no sooner made than marred –
Half-men, whom many a rich and noble dame,
To serve her lust, and yet secure her fame,
Keeps on high diet, as we capons feed,
240 To glut our appetites at last decreed,
Women, who dance, in postures so obscene,
They might awaken shame in Aretine,
Who, when, retired from the day's piercing light,
They celebrate the mysteries of night,
245 Might make the Muses, in a corner placed
To view their monstrous lusts, deem Sappho chaste;
These, and a thousand follies rank as these,
A thousand faults, ten thousand fools, who please
Our palled and sickly taste, ten thousand knaves,
250 Who serve our foes as spies, and us as slaves,
Who by degrees, and unperceived, prepare
Our necks for chains which they already wear,
Madly we entertain, at the expense
Of fame, of virtue, taste, and common-sense.

255   Nor stop we here – the soft luxurious East,
Where man, his soul degraded, from the beast
In nothing different but in shape we view,
They walk on four legs, and he walks on two,
Attracts our eye, and, flowing from that source,
260 Sins of the blackest character, sins worse
Than all her plagues, which truly to unfold
Would make the best blood in my veins run cold,
And strike all manhood dead, which but to name
Would call up in my cheeks the marks of shame,

265 Sins, if such sins can be, which shut out grace,
     Which for the guilty leave no hope, no place
     E'en in God's mercy, sins 'gainst Nature's plan
     Possess the land at large, and man for man
     Burns in those fires, which Hell alone could raise
270 To make him more than damned, which, in the days
     Of punishment, when guilt becomes her prey,
     With all her tortures she can scarce repay.

     Be Grace shut out, be Mercy deaf, let God
     With tenfold terrors arm that dreadful nod
275 Which speaks them lost, and sentenced to despair;
     Distending wide her jaws, let Hell prepare
     For those who thus offend amongst mankind,
     A fire more fierce, and tortures more refined;
     On earth, which groans beneath their monstrous weight,
280 On earth, alas! They meet a different fate,
     And whilst the laws, false grace, false mercy shown,
     Are taught to wear a softness not their own,
     Men, whom the beasts would spurn, should they appear
     Amongst the honest herd, find refuge here.

285   No longer by vain fear, or shame controlled,
     From long, too long security grown bold,
     Mocking rebuke, they brave it in our streets,
     And Lumley e'en at noon his mistress meets.
     So public in their crimes, so daring grown,
290 They almost take a pride to have them known,
     And each unnatural villain scarce endures
     To make a secret of his vile amours.
     Go where we will, at every time and place,
     Sodom confronts, and stares us in the face;
295 They ply in public at our very doors
     And take the bread from much more honest whores.
     Those who are mean high paramours secure,
     And the rich guilty screen the guilty poor;
     The sin too proud to feel from reason awe,
300 And those, who practise it, too great for Law.

Woman, the pride and happiness of man,
Without whose soft endearments Nature's plan
Had been a blank, and life not worth a thought;
Woman, by all the loves and graces taught,
305 With softest arts, and sure, though hidden skill
To humanise, and mould us to her will;
Woman, with more than common grace formed here,
With the persuasive language of a tear
To melt the rugged temper of our isle,
310 Or win us to her purpose with a smile;
Woman, by fate the quickest spur decreed,
The fairest, best reward of every deed
Which bears the stamp of honour, at whose name
Our ancient heroes caught a quicker flame,
315 And dared beyond belief, whilst o'er the plain,
Spurning the carcases of princes slain,
Confusion proudly strode, whilst Horror blew
The fatal trump, and Death stalked full in view;
Woman is out of date, a thing thrown by
320 As having lost its use; no more the eye
With female beauty caught, in wild amaze,
Gazes entranced, and could for ever gaze;
No more the heart, that seat where Love resides,
Each breath drawn quick and short, in fuller tides
325 Life posting through the veins, each pulse on fire,
And the whole body tingling with desire,
Pants for those charms, which Virtue might engage
To break his vow, and thaw the frost of age,
Bidding each trembling nerve, each muscle strain,
330 And giving pleasure which is almost pain.
Women are kept for nothing but the breed;
For pleasure we must have a Ganymede,
A fine, fresh Hylas, a delicious boy,
To serve our purposes of beastly joy.

335 Fairest of nymphs, where every nymph is fair,
Whom Nature formed with more than common care,
With more than common care whom Art improved,
And both declared most worthy to be loved,

[Aynam] neglected wanders, whilst a crowd
340 Pursue, and consecrate the steps [of Stroud.]
She, hapless maid, born in a wretched hour,
Wastes life's gay prime in vain, like some fair flower,
Sweet in its scent, and lively in its hue,
Which withers on the stalk from whence it grew,
345 And dies uncropped, whilst he, admired, caressed,
Beloved, and everywhere a welcome guest,
With brutes of rank and fortune plays the whore,
For their unnatural lust a common sewer.

Dine with Apicius – at his sumptuous board
350 Find all the world of dainties can afford –
And yet (so much distempered spirits pall
The sickly appetite) amidst them all
Apicius finds no joy, but, whilst he carves
For every guest, the landlord sits and starves.

355 The forest haunch, fine, fat, in flavour high,
Kept to a moment, smokes before his eye,
But smokes in vain; his heedless eye runs o'er
And loathes what he had deified before;
The turtle, of a great and glorious size,
360 Worth its own weight in gold, a mighty prize
For which a man of taste all risks would run,
Itself a feast, and every dish in one,
The turtle in luxurious pomp comes in,
Kept, killed, cut up, prepared, and dressed by Quin;
365 In vain it comes, in vain lies full in view;
As Quin hath dressed it, he may eat it too,
Apicius cannot – when the glass goes round,
Quick circling, and the roofs with mirth resound,
Sober he sits, and silent – all alone
370 Though in a crowd, and to himself scarce known,
On grief he feeds, nor friends can cure, nor wine
Suspend his cares, and make him cease to pine.

Why mourns Apicius thus? why runs his eye,
Heedless, o'er delicates, which from the sky

375 Might call down Jove? Where now his generous wish
     That, to invent a new and better dish,
     The world might burn, and all mankind expire,
     So he might roast a phoenix at the fire.
     Why swims that eye in tears, which, through a race
380 Of sixty years, ne'er showed one sign of grace?
     Why feels that heart, which never felt before?
     Why doth that pampered glutton eat no more,
     Who only lived to eat, his stomach palled,
     And drowned in floods of sorrow? hath Fate called
385 His father from the grave to second life?
     Hath Clodius on his hands returned his wife,
     Or hath the Law, by strictest justice taught,
     Compelled him to restore the dower she brought?
     Hath some bold creditor against his will
390 Brought in, and forced him to discharge a bill,
     Where eating had no share? Hath some vain wench
     Run out his wealth, and forced him to retrench?
     Hath any rival glutton got the start,
     And beat him in his own luxurious art,
395 Bought cates for which Apicius could not pay,
     Or dressed old dainties in a newer way?
     Hath his cook, worthy to be slain with rods,
     Spoiled a dish, fit to entertain the gods,
     Or hath some varlet, crossed by cruel Fate,
400 Thrown down the price of empires in a plate?

          None, none of these – his servants all are tried,
     So sure, they walk on ice, and never slide;
     His cook, an acquisition made in France,
     Might put a Chloe out of countenance,
405 Nor, though old Holles still maintains his stand,
     Hath he one rival glutton in the land;
     Women are all the objects of his hate,
     His debts are all unpaid, and yet his state
     In full security and triumph held,
410 Unless for once a knave should be expelled;
     His wife is still a whore, and in his power,
     The woman gone, he still retains the dower;

Sound in the grave (thanks to his filial care
Which mixed the draught, and kindly sent him there),
415   His father sleeps, and, till the last trump shake
The corners of the earth, shall not awake.

Whence flows this sorrow then? behind his chair
Did'st thou not see, decked with a solitaire
Which on his bare breast glittering played, and graced
420   With nicest ornaments, a stripling placed,
A smooth, smug stripling in life's fairest prime?
Did'st thou not mind too, how from time to time,
The monstrous lecher, tempted to despise
All other dainties, thither turned his eyes?
425   How he seem'd inly to reproach us all,
Who strove his fixed attention to recall,
And how he wished, e'en at the time of grace,
Like Janus, to have had a double face?
His cause of grief behold in that fair boy;
430   Apicius dotes, and Corydon is coy.

Vain and unthinking stripling! When the glass
Meets thy too curious eye, and, as you pass,
Flattering, presents in smiles thy image there,
Why dost thou bless the gods, who made thee fair?
435   Blame their large bounties, and with reason blame;
Curse, curse thy beauty, for it leads to shame.
When thy hot Lord, to work thee to his end,
Bids showers of gold into thy breast descend,
Suspect his gifts, nor the vile giver trust;
440   They're baits for Virtue, and smell strong of lust.
On those gay, gaudy trappings, which adorn
The temple of thy body, look with scorn,
View them with horror, they pollution mean
And deepest ruin; thou hast often seen,
445   From 'mongst the herd, the fairest and the best
Carefully singled out, and richly dressed,
With grandeur mocked, for sacrifice decreed,
Only in greater pomp at last to bleed.

Be warned in time, the threatened danger shun,
450   To stay a moment is to be undone.
What though, temptation-proof, thy virtue shine,
Nor bribes can move, nor arts can undermine,
All other methods failing, one resource
Is still behind, and thou must yield to force.
455   Paint to thyself the horrors of a rape,
Most strongly paint, and, while thou can'st escape,
Mind not his promises – they're made in sport –
Made to be broke – was he not bred at Court?
Trust not his honour; he's a man of birth;
460   Attend not to his oaths – they're made on earth,
Not registered in Heaven – he mocks at grace,
And in his creed God never found a place –
Look not for Conscience – for he knows her not,
So long a stranger, she is quite forgot –
465   Nor think thyself in Law secure and firm –
Thy master is a Lord, and thou a worm,
A poor mean reptile, never meant to think,
Who, being well supplied with meat and drink,
And suffered just to crawl from place to place,
470   Must serve his lusts, and think he does thee grace.

Fly then, whilst yet 'tis in thy power to fly,
But whither can'st thou go? on whom rely
For wished protection? Virtue's sure to meet
An armed host of foes, in every street.
475   What boots it, of Apicius fearful grown,
Headlong to fly into the arms of Stone,
Or why take refuge in the house of prayer,
If sure to meet with an Apicius there?
Trust not old age, which will thy faith betray;
480   Saint Socrates is still a goat, though grey;
Trust not green youth; Florio will scarce go down,
And, at eighteen, hath surfeited the town;
Trust not to rakes – alas! 'tis all pretence –
They take up raking only as a fence
485   'Gainst common fame – place H[ervey] in thy view;
He keeps one whore, as Barrowby kept two;

Trust not to marriage – T— took a wife,
Who chaste as Dian might have passed her life,
Had she not, far more prudent in her aim,
490 (To propagate the honours of his name,
And save expiring titles) taken care
Without his knowledge to provide an heir;
Trust not to marriage, in mankind unread;
S[ackville]'s a married man, and S[troud] new wed.

495   Would'st thou be safe? Society forswear,
Fly to the desert, and seek shelter there,
Herd with the brutes – they follow Nature's plan –
There's not one brute so dangerous as man
In Afric's wilds – 'mongst them that refuge find,
500 Which Lust denies thee here among mankind;
Renounce thy name, thy nature, and no more
Pique thy vain pride on manhood, on all four
Walk, as you see those honest creatures do,
And quite forget that once you walked on two.

505   But, if the thoughts of solitude alarm,
And social life hath one remaining charm,
If still thou art to jeopardy decreed
Amongst the monsters of Augusta's breed,
Lay by thy sex, thy safety to procure;
510 Put off the man, from men to live secure;
Go forth a woman to the public view,
And with their garb assume their manners too.
Had the light footed Greek of Chiron's school
Been wise enough to keep this single rule,
515 The maudlin hero, like a puling boy
Robbed of his play-thing, on the plains of Troy
Had never blubbered at Patroclus' tomb,
And placed his minion in his mistress' room.
Be not in this than catamites more nice,
520 Do that for virtue, which they do for vice.
Thus shalt thou pass untainted life's gay bloom,
Thus stand uncourted in the drawing room,

At midnight thus, untempted, walk the street,
And run no danger but of being beat.

525   Where is the mother, whose officious zeal
Discreetly judging what her daughters feel
By what she felt herself in days of yore,
Against that lecher man makes fast the door,
Who not permits, e'en for the sake of prayer,
530 A priest, uncastrated, to enter there,
Nor (could her wishes, and her care prevail)
Would suffer in the house a fly that's male?
Let her discharge her cares, throw wide her doors,
Her daughters cannot, if they would, be whores,
535 Nor can a man be found, as times now go,
Who thinks it worth his while to make them so.

     Though they, more fresh, more lively than the morn,
And brighter than the noon-day sun, adorn
The works of Nature, though the mother's grace
540 Revives, improved, in every daughter's face,
Undisciplined in dull discretion's rules,
Untaught, and undebauch'd by boarding schools,
Free and unguarded, let them range the town,
Go forth at random, and run pleasure down;
545 Start where she will, discard all taint of fear,
Nor think of danger, when no danger's near.
Watch not their steps – they're safe without thy care,
Unless, like jennets, they conceive by air,
And every one of them may die a nun,
550 Unless they breed, like carrion, in the sun.
Men, dead to pleasure, as they're dead to grace,
Against the law of Nature set their face,
The grand, primeval law, and seem combined
To stop the propagation of mankind;
555 Vile pathicks read the marriage act with pride,
And fancy that the Law is on their side.

     Broke down, and Strength a stranger to his bed,
Old L[igonier], though yet alive, is dead;

T[yrawley] lives no more, or lives not to our isle;
560 No longer blessed with a Cz[arina]'s smile
T[yrawley] is at P[etersburgh] disgraced,
And M[ontagu] grown grey, perforce grows chaste;
Nor, to the credit of our modest race,
Rises one stallion to supply their place.
565 A maidenhead, which, twenty years ago,
In mid-December, the rank fly would blow
Though closely kept, now, when the dog-star's heat
Enflames the marrow, in the very street
May lie untouched, left for the worms, by those
570 Who daintily pass by, and hold their nose.
Poor, plain Concupiscence is in disgrace,
And simple Lechery dares not show her face
Lest she be sent to Bridewell; bankrupts made,
To save their fortunes, bawds leave off that trade,
575 Which first had left off them; to Well-close Square
Fine, fresh, young strumpets (for Dodd preaches there)
Throng for subsistence; pimps no longer thrive,
And pensions only keep L[igonier] alive.

Where is the mother, who thinks all her pain,
580 And all her jeopardy of travail, gain,
When a man child is born, thinks every prayer
Paid to the full, and answered in an heir?
Shortsighted woman! Little doth she know
What streams of sorrow from that source may flow,
585 Little suspect, whilst she surveys her boy,
Her young Narcissus, with an eye of joy
Too full for continence, that Fate could give
Her darling as a curse, that she may live,
E're sixteen winters their short course have run,
590 In agonies of soul, to curse that son.

Pray then for daughters, ye wise mothers, pray;
They shall reward your love, nor make ye grey
Before your time with sorrow; they shall give
Ages of peace and comfort, whilst ye live

595   Make life most truly worth your care, and save,
      In spite of death, your memories from the grave.

          That sense, with more than manly vigour fraught,
      That fortitude of soul, that stretch of thought,
      That genius, great beyond the narrow bound
600   Of earth's low walk, that judgment perfect found,
      When wanted most, that purity of taste,
      Which critics mention by the name of chaste,
      Adorned with elegance, that easy flow
      Of ready wit, which never made a foe,
605   That face, that form, that dignity, that ease,
      Those powers of pleasing with that will to please,
      By which Lepel, when in her youthful days,
      E'en from the currish Pope extorted praise,
      We see, transmitted, in her daughter shine,
610   And view a new Lepel in Caroline.

          Is a son born into this world of woe?
      In never-ceasing streams let sorrow flow,
      Be from that hour the house with sables hung,
      Let lamentations dwell upon thy tongue,
615   E'en from the moment that he first began
      To wail and whine, let him not see a man.
      Lock, lock him up, far from the public eye,
      Give him no opportunity to buy,
      Or to be bought; B—, though rich, was sold,
620   And gave his body up to shame for gold.

          Let it be bruited all about the town,
      That he is coarse, indelicate, and brown,
      An antidote to lust, his face deep scarred
      With the smallpox, his body maimed and marred,
625   Eat up with the kings-evil, and his blood,
      Tainted throughout, a thick and putrid flood,
      Where dwells corruption, making him all o'er,
      From head to foot, a rank and running sore.
      Should'st thou report him as by Nature made,
630   He is undone, and by thy praise betrayed;

Give him out fair, lechers in number more,
More brutal and more fierce, than thronged the door
Of Lot in Sodom, shall to thine repair,
And force a passage, though a god is there.

635   Let him not have one servant that is male;
Where Lords are baffled, servants oft prevail.
Some vices they propose, to all agree;
H— was guilty, but was M— free?

Give him no tutor – throw him to a punk,
640   Rather than trust his morals to a monk –
Monks we all know – we, who have lived at home,
From fair report, and travellers, who roam,
More feelingly – nor trust him to the gown,
'Tis oft a covering in this vile town
645   For base designs; ourselves have lived to see
More than one parson in the pillory.
Should he have brothers (image to thy view
A scene, which though not public made, is true),
Let not one brother be to t'other known,
650   Nor let his father sit with him alone.

Be all his servants, female, young, and fair,
And if the pride of Nature spur thy heir
To deeds of venery, if, hot and wild,
He chance to get some score of maids with child,
655   Chide, but forgive him; whoredom is a crime,
Which, more at this, than any other time,
Calls for indulgence, and, 'mongst such a race,
To have a bastard is some sign of grace.

Born in such times, should I sit tamely down,
660   Suppress my rage, and saunter through the town
As one who knew not, or who shared these crimes?
Should I at lesser evils point my rhymes,
And let this giant sin, in the full eye
Of observation, pass unwounded by?

665   Though our meek wives, passive obedience taught,
       Patiently bear those wrongs, for which they ought,
       With the brave spirit of their dams possessed,
       To plant a dagger in each husband's breast,
       To cut off male increase from this fair isle,
670   And turn our Thames into another Nile;
       Though, on his Sunday, the smug pulpiteer,
       Loud 'gainst all other crimes, is silent here,
       And thinks himself absolved, in the pretence
       Of decency, which meant for the defence
675   Of real Virtue, and to raise her price,
       Becomes an agent for the cause of Vice;
       Though the Law sleeps, and, through the care they take
       To drug her well, may never more awake;
       Born in such times, nor with that patience cursed
680   Which saints may boast of, I must speak, or burst.

       But if, too eager in my bold career,
       Haply I wound the nice, and chaster ear,
       If, all unguarded, all too rude, I speak,
       And call up blushes in the maiden's cheek,
685   Forgive, ye fair – my real motives view,
       And to forgiveness add your praises too.
       For you I write – nor wish a better plan –
       The cause of woman is most worthy man –
       For you I still will write, nor hold my hand,
690   Whilst there's one slave of Sodom in the land.

       Let them fly far, and skulk from place to place,
       Not daring to meet manhood face to face,
       Their steps I'll track, nor yield them one retreat
       Where they may hide their heads, or rest their feet,
695   Till God in wrath shall let his vengeance fall,
       And make a great example of them all,
       Bidding in one grand pile this town expire,
       Her towers in dust, her Thames a lake of fire,
       Or they (most worth our wish) convinced, though late,
700   Of their past crimes, and dangerous estate,
       Pardon of women with repentance buy,
       And learn to honour them, as much as I.

The Journey: A Fragment

Some of my friends (for friends I must suppose
All, who, not daring to appear my foes,
Feign great good will, and, not more full of spite
Than full of craft, under false colours fight)
5   Some of my friends (so lavishly I print)
As more in sorrow than in anger, hint
(Though that indeed will scarce admit a doubt)
That I shall run my stock of genius out,
My no great stock, and, publishing so fast,
10   Must needs become a bankrupt at the last.

'The Husbandman, to spare a thankful soil,
Which, rich in disposition, pays his toil
More than a hundred-fold, which swells his store
E'en to his wish, and makes his barns run o'er,
15   By long experience taught, who teaches best,
Forgoes his hopes awhile, and gives it rest.
The land, allowed its losses to repair,
Refreshed, and full in strength, delights to wear
A second youth, and to the farmer's eyes
20   Bids richer crops, and double harvests rise.

'Nor think this practice to the earth confined,
It reaches to the culture of the mind.
The mind of man craves rest, and cannot bear,
Though next in power to gods, continual care.
25   Genius himself (nor here let Genius frown)
Must, to ensure his vigour, be laid down,
And fallowed well; had Churchill known but this,
Which the most slight observer scarce could miss,
He might have flourished twenty years, or more,
30   Though now alas! poor man! worn out in four.'

Recovered from the vanity of youth,
I feel, alas! this melancholy truth,

Thanks to each cordial, each advising friend,
And am, if not too late, resolved to mend,
35 Resolved to give some respite to my pen,
Apply myself once more to books, and men,
View what is present, what is past review,
And, my old stock exhausted, lay in new.
For twice six moons (let winds, turned porters, bear
40 This oath to Heaven) for twice six moons I swear,
No Muse shall tempt me with her siren lay,
Nor draw me from improvement's thorny way.
Verse I abjure, nor will forgive that friend,
Who in my hearing shall a rhyme commend.

45   It cannot be – Whether I will, or no,
Such as they are, my thoughts in measure flow.
Convinced, determined, I in prose begin,
But e're I write one sentence, verse creeps in,
And taints me through and through; by this good light
50 In verse I talk by day, I dream by night;
If now and then I curse, my curses chime,
Nor can I pray, unless I pray in rhyme.
E'en now I err, in spite of common sense,
And my confession doubles my offence.

55   Rest then my friends – spare, spare your precious breath,
And be your slumbers not less sound than death;
Perturbed spirits rest, nor thus appear
To waste your counsels in a spendthrift's ear;
On your grave lessons I cannot subsist,
60 Nor e'en in verse become Economist;
Rest then my friends, nor, hateful to my eyes,
Let Envy, in the shape of Pity, rise
To blast me e're my time; with patience wait
('Tis no long interval), propitious Fate
65 Shall glut your pride, and every son of phlegm
Find ample room to censure and condemn.
Read some three hundred lines (no easy task;
But probably the last that I shall ask),

And give me up for ever; wait one hour,
70 Nay not so much, revenge is in your power,
And ye may cry, e're Time hath turned his glass,
Lo! what we prophesied is come to pass.

Let those, who poetry in poems claim,
Or not read this, or only read to blame;
75 Let those, who are by fiction's charms enslaved,
Return me thanks for half a crown well-saved;
Let those, who love a little gall in rhyme,
Postpone their purchase now, and call next time;
Let those, who, void of Nature, look for art,
80 Take up their money, and in peace depart;
Let those, who energy of diction prize,
For Billingsgate quit Flexney, and be wise;
Here is no lie, no gall, no art, no force,
Mean are the words, and such as come of course,
85 The subject not less simple than the lay;
A plain, unlaboured journey of a day.

Far from me now be every tuneful maid,
I neither ask, nor can receive their aid.
Pegasus turned into a common hack,
90 Alone I jog, and keep the beaten track,
Nor would I have the sisters of the hill
Behold their bard in such a dishabille.
Absent, but only absent for a time,
Let them caress some dearer son of rhyme,
95 Let them, as far as decency permits,
Without suspicion, play the fool with wits,
'Gainst fools be guarded; 'tis a certain rule,
Wits are safe things, there's danger in a fool.

Let them, though modest, Gray more modest woo;
100 Let them with Mason bleat, and bray, and coo;
Let them with Francklin, proud of some small Greek,
Make Sophocles, disguised, in English speak;
Let them with Glover o'er Medea doze;
Let them with Dodsley wail Cleone's woes,

105 Whilst he, fine feeling creature, all in tears,
    Melts as they melt, and weeps with weeping peers;
    Let them with simple Whitehead, taught to creep
    Silent and soft, lay Fontenelle asleep;
    Let them with Brown contrive, no vulgar trick,
110 To cure the dead, and make the living sick;
    Let them in charity to Murphy give
    Some old French piece, that he may steal and live;
    Let them with antic Foote subscriptions get,
    And advertise a summer-house of wit.

115   Thus, or in any better way they please,
    With these great men, or with great men like these,
    Let them their appetite for laughter feed;
    I on my journey all alone proceed.

        If fashionable grown, and fond of power
120 With humorous Scots let them disport their hour;
    Let them dance, fairy-like, round Ossian's tomb;
    Let them forge lies, and histories for Hume;
    Let them with Home, the very prince of verse,
    Make something like a tragedy in Erse;
125 Under dark Allegory's flimsy veil
    Let them with Ogilvie spin out a tale
    Of rueful length; let them plain things obscure,
    Debase what's truly rich, and what is poor
    Make poorer still by jargon most uncouth;
130 With every pert, prim prettiness of youth
    Born of false taste, with fancy (like a child
    Not knowing what it cries for) running wild,
    With bloated style, by Affectation taught,
    With much false colouring, and little thought,
135 With phrases strange, and dialect decreed
    By reason never to have passed the Tweed,
    With words, which Nature meant each other's foe,
    Forced to compound whether they will or no,
    With such materials, let them, if they will,
140 To prove at once their pleasantry and skill,

Build up a bard to war 'gainst common sense,
By way of compliment to Providence;
Let them with Armstrong, taking leave of sense,
Read musty lectures on *Benevolence*,
145 Or con the pages of his gaping *Day*,
Where all his former fame was thrown away,
Where all, but barren labour, was forgot,
And the vain stiffness of a lettered Scot;
Let them with Armstrong pass the term of light,
150 But not one hour of darkness; when the night
Suspends this mortal coil, when Memory wakes,
When for our past misdoings Conscience takes
A deep revenge, when, by Reflection led,
She draws his curtains, and looks comfort dead,
155 Let every Muse be gone; in vain he turns
And tries to pray for sleep; an Etna burns,
A more than Etna in his coward breast,
And Guilt, with vengeance armed, forbids him rest.
Though soft as plumage from young Zephyr's wing,
160 His couch seems hard, and no relief can bring.
Ingratitude hath planted daggers there,
No good man can deserve, no brave man bear.

Thus, or in any better way they please,
With these great men, or with great men like these,
165 Let them their appetite for laughter feed;
I on my journey all alone proceed.

WILLIAM COWPER

Poems

A NOTE ON THE TEXT

Cowper's poems present complex editorial problems, and the interested reader should consult the magisterial and lucid scholarship of John D. Baird and Charles Ryskamp, editors of *The Poems of William Cowper* (3 vols., Oxford, 1980–95; an unmodernized text), to which I am greatly indebted. It would be perverse to depart significantly from their editorial principles.

For the purposes of this selection, some general textual points need to be made. Cowper's poems were published in three main editions in his lifetime, which are the main source of copy text in the following selection: the *Olney Hymns, in Three Books* (with John Newton) in 1779; *Poems by William Cowper, of the Inner Temple, Esq.* in 1782; and *The Task* in 1785. A large number of Cowper's poems, however, were not published until after his death. Many were published in William Hayley's *The Life, and Posthumous Writings, of William Cowper, Esqr.* (3 vols., 1803–4); others by Cowper's cousin, John Johnson, in volume three of the collected *Poems, by William Cowper, of the Inner Temple, Esq.* (3 vols., 1815); and still others in *Poems, the Early Productions of William Cowper, Now First Published from the Originals in the Possession of James Croft* (1825), Croft being the great-nephew of Cowper's cousin Theadora Cowper. One of the poems selected here, 'Hatred and Vengeance, My Eternal Portion', was first printed in *Memoirs of the Most Remarkable and Interesting Parts of the Life of William Cowper*, edited by E. Cox in 1816.

For poems not published in Cowper's own lifetime for which manuscripts survive, copy text derives from the latest version of the manuscript which Cowper oversaw, or which is otherwise reliable. If no manuscript exists, copy text derives from the most authoritative early published version.

To C.P., Ill with the Rheumatism

Could mine, my friend, like Orpheus' pleasing strain,
Charm the keen anguish of tormenting pain,
Could I the sharp rheumatic grief assuage,
And bid the raging humour cease to rage,
5   Straight should my lines the wished-for ease impart
And the kind poet, play the doctor's part.

And wherefore, Phoebus, since to thee mankind
Have the two precious attributes assigned,
Medicine to heal, and music to delight,
10   Why not in one these glorious ends unite?
Why not on verse the various powers bestow,
That please our ear, and mitigate our woe?
So should the sick some well wrote page survey,
Smile while he reads and bless the saving lay!
15   So should smooth verse o'er every pang prevail
And Pope succeed, where haply Mead might fail.
'If rising vapours fill your aching head,
Trust me, let Swift's, or Butler's page be read;
Wouldst thou confirm the cure, my friend, at least
20   Five acts of Shakespeare take, *probatum est*!
If sleepless nights your wandering thoughts confound,
In Blackmore's page much opiate may be found;
E'en Garth though dead shall thy physician be,
And still more wondrous! cure without a fee!'
25   Methinks I see your heavy eyelids close;
Lo! for a while my friend forgets his woes,
Though Phoebus does the healing art deny
To tuneful bards, and though no bard am I,
Yet may this verse thy torturing grief allay,
30   Benumb thy sense, and charm the pain away.
Oh, were I sure that glorious end to gain,
Torpedo-like to free thy limbs from pain!
Plenteous my numbers should for ever flow,
Nor peace my brain, nor rest my fingers know;

35   Then should'st thou yawning their soft influence own,
     And let the purpose for the faults atone;
     Then should'st thou drop the leaf, forget thy pain,
     And doze, and wake, and read, and doze again.

     Grant me the muse, ye gods! whose humble flight
40   Seeks not the mountain-top's pernicious height!
     Who can the tall Parnassian cliff forsake,
     To visit oft the still Lethean lake,
     Now her slow pinions brush the silent shore,
     Now gently skim the unwrinkled waters o'er,
45   There dips her downy plumes, then upward flies
     And sheds soft slumbers in her votary's eyes:
     My prayers are heard; I feel the lulling power
     O'erload my brain, my lazy sense obscure –
     Adieu my friend! may slumbers mild as these,
50   The raging anguish of thy limbs appease,
     Success attend my prayers, be thine preferred
     To the same power, and share the same reward.

'This Evening, Delia, You and I'

     This evening, Delia, you and I
     Have managed most delightfully,
          For with a frown we parted;
     Having contrived some trifle that
5   We both may be much troubled at,
          And sadly disconcerted.

     Yet well as each performed their part,
     We might perceive it was but art;
          And that we both intended
10   To sacrifice a little ease;
     For all such petty flaws as these
          Are made but to be mended.

You knew, dissembler! all the while,
How sweet it was to reconcile
  After this heavy pelt;
That we should gain by this allay
When next we met, and laugh away
  The care we never felt.

Happy! when we but seem t'endure
A little pain, then find a cure
  By double joy requited;
For friendship, like a severed bone,
Improves and gains a stronger tone
  When aptly reunited.

'Hope, Like the Short-lived Ray that Gleams Awhile'

Hope, like the short-lived ray that gleams awhile
  Through wintry skies upon the frozen waste,
Cheers e'en the face of misery to a smile;
  But soon the momentary pleasure's past!

How oft, my Delia! since our last farewell
  (Years that have rolled since that distressful hour),
Grieved I have said, when most our hopes prevail,
  Our promised happiness is least secure.

Oft I have thought the scene of troubles closed,
  And hoped once more to gaze upon your charms;
As oft some dire mischance has interposed,
  And snatched the expected blessing from my arms.

The seaman thus, his shattered vessel lost,
  Still vainly strives to shun the threatening death;
And while he thinks to gain the friendly coast,
  And drops his feet, and feels the sands beneath,

Borne by the wave, steep-sloping from the shore,
  Back to the inclement deep, again he beats
The surge aside, and seems to tread secure;
20   And now the refluent wave his baffled toil defeats.

Had you, my love, forbade me to pursue
  My fond attempt, disdainfully retired,
And with proud scorn compelled me to subdue
  Th' ill-fated passion by yourself inspired;

25 Then haply to some distant spot removed,
  Hopeless to gain, unwilling to molest
With fond entreaties whom I dearly loved,
  Despair or absence had redeemed my rest.

But now, sole partner in my Delia's heart,
30 Yet doomed far off in exile to complain,
Eternal absence cannot ease my smart,
  And hope subsists but to prolong my pain.

Oh then! kind heaven, be this my latest breath;
  Here end my life, or make it worth my care;
35 Absence from whom we love is worse than death,
  And frustrate hope severer than despair.

'Doomed, as I am, in Solitude to Waste'

Doomed, as I am, in solitude to waste
The present moments, and regret the past;
Deprived of every joy I valued most,
My friend torn from me, and my mistress lost;
5 Call not this gloom I wear, this anxious mien,
The dull effect of humour, or of spleen!
Still, still, I mourn, with each returning day,
Him snatched by Fate, in early youth, away.
And her – through tedious years of doubt and pain,
10 Fixed in her choice, and faithful – but in vain!

Oh prone to pity, generous, and sincere,
Whose eye ne'er yet refused the wretch a tear;
Whose heart the real claim of friendship knows,
Nor thinks a lover's are but fancied woes;
15 See me – e're yet my destined course half done,
Cast forth a wanderer on a wild unknown!
See me neglected on the world's rude coast,
Each dear companion of my voyage lost!
Nor ask why clouds of sorrow shade my brow!
20 And ready tears wait only leave to flow!
Why all that soothes a heart, from anguish free,
All that delights the happy – palls with me!

Light Shining out of Darkness

(HYMN 35, from *Olney Hymns*)

God moves in a mysterious way,
His wonders to perform,
He plants his footsteps in the sea,
And rides upon the storm.

5 Deep in unfathomable mines,
Of never failing skill,
He treasures up his bright designs,
And works his sovereign will.

Ye fearful saints fresh courage take,
10 The clouds ye so much dread,
Are big with mercy, and shall break
In blessings on your head.

Judge not the Lord by feeble sense,
But trust him for his grace,
15 Behind a frowning providence
He hides a smiling face.

His purposes will ripen fast,
Unfolding every hour,
The bud may have a bitter taste,
20 But sweet will be the flower.

Blind unbelief is sure to err,
And scan his work in vain,
God is his own interpreter,
And he will make it plain.

Temptation

(HYMN 38, from *Olney Hymns*)

The billows swell, the winds are high,
Clouds overcast my wintry sky;
Out of the depths to thee I call,
My fears are great, my strength is small.

5 O Lord, the pilot's part perform,
And guide and guard me through the storm;
Defend me from each threatening ill,
Control the waves, say, 'Peace, be still.'

Amidst the roaring of the sea,
10 My soul still hangs her hope on thee,
Thy constant love, thy faithful care,
Is all that saves me from despair.

Dangers of every shape and name
Attend the followers of the Lamb,
15 Who leave the world's deceitful shore,
And leave it to return no more.

Though tempest-tossed and half a wreck,
My Saviour through the floods I seek;
Let neither winds nor stormy main,
20 Force back my shattered bark again.

Retirement

(HYMN 47, from *Olney Hymns*)

Far from the world, oh Lord I flee,
From strife and tumult far,
From scenes where Satan wages still
His most successful war.

5   The calm retreat, the silent shade,
With prayer and praise agree;
And seem, by thy sweet bounty made,
For those who follow thee.

There, if thy spirit touch the soul,
10   And grace her mean abode;
Oh with what peace, and joy, and love,
She communes with her God!

There, like the nightingale she pours
Her solitary lays;
15   Nor asks a witness of her song,
Nor thirsts for human praise.

Author and guardian of my life,
Sweet source of light divine!
And all harmonious names, in *One*,
20   *My Saviour* – thou art mine!

What thanks I owe thee, and what love,
A boundless, endless store;
Shall echo through the realms above,
When time shall be no more.

'Hatred and Vengeance, My Eternal Portion'

Hatred and vengeance, my eternal portion,
Scarce can endure delay of execution:–
Wait, with impatient readiness, to seize my
    Soul in a moment.
5   Damned below Judas; more abhorred than he was,
Who, for a few pence, sold his holy master.
Twice betrayed, Jesus me, the last delinquent,
    Deems the profanest.
Man disavows, and deity disowns me.
10 Hell might afford my miseries a shelter;
Therefore hell keeps her everhungry mouths all
    Bolted against me.
Hard lot! Encompassed with a thousand dangers,
Weary, faint, trembling with a thousand terrors,
15 I'm called, if vanquished, to receive a sentence
    Worse than Abiram's:
Him, the vindictive rod of angry justice
Sent, quick and howling, to the centre headlong;
I, fed with judgments, in a fleshly tomb, am
20   Buried above ground.

The Bee and the Pineapple

A bee allured by the perfume
Of a rich pineapple in bloom,
Found it within a frame enclosed,
And licked the glass that interposed.
5   Blossoms of apricot and peach,
The flowers that blowed within his reach,
Were arrant drugs compared with that
He strove so vainly to get at.
No rose could yield so rare a treat,
10 Nor jessamine was half so sweet.

The gardener saw this much ado,
(The gardener was the master too)
And thus he said – 'Poor restless bee!
I learn philosophy from thee –
15 I learn how just it is and wise,
To use what Providence supplies,
To leave fine titles, lordships, graces,
Rich pensions, dignities and places,
Those gifts of a superior kind,
20 To those for whom they were designed.
I learn that comfort dwells alone
In that which Heaven has made our own,
That fools incur no greater pain
Than pleasure coveted in vain.'

To Mr Newton on His Return from Ramsgate

That ocean you of late surveyed,
      Those rocks I too have seen,
But I, afflicted and dismayed,
      You tranquil and serene.

5   You from the flood-controlling steep
      Saw stretched before your view,
With conscious joy, the threatening deep,
      No longer such to you.

To me, the waves that ceaseless broke
10   Upon the dangerous coast,
Hoarsely and ominously spoke
      Of all my treasure lost.

Your sea of troubles you have passed,
      And found the peaceful shore;
15 I tempest-tossed and wrecked at last,
      Come home to port no more.

Verses, Supposed to be Written by Alexander Selkirk

DURING HIS SOLITARY ABODE IN THE ISLAND OF JUAN FERNANDEZ

I am monarch of all I survey,
    My right there is none to dispute,
From the centre all round to the sea,
    I am lord of the fowl and the brute.
5 Oh solitude! where are the charms
    That sages have seen in thy face?
Better dwell in the midst of alarms,
    Than reign in this horrible place.

I am out of humanity's reach,
10   I must finish my journey alone,
Never hear the sweet music of speech,
    I start at the sound of my own.
The beasts that roam over the plain,
    My form with indifference see,
15 They are so unacquainted with man,
    Their tameness is shocking to me.

Society, friendship, and love,
    Divinely bestowed upon man,
Oh had I the wings of a dove,
20   How soon would I taste you again!
My sorrows I then might assuage,
    In the ways of religion and truth,
Might learn from the wisdom of age,
    And be cheered by the sallies of youth.

25 Religion! what treasure untold
    Resides in that heavenly word!
More precious than silver and gold,
    Or all that this earth can afford.

But the sound of the church-going bell
  These vallies and rocks never heard,
Ne'er sighed at the sound of a knell,
  Or smiled when a sabbath appeared.

Ye winds that have made me your sport,
  Convey to this desolate shore,
Some cordial endearing report
  Of a land I shall visit no more.
My friends do they now and then send
  A wish or a thought after me?
O tell me I yet have a friend,
  Though a friend I am never to see.

How fleet is a glance of the mind!
  Compared with the speed of its flight,
The tempest itself lags behind,
  And the swift wingèd arrows of light.
When I think of my own native land,
  In a moment I seem to be there;
But alas! recollection at hand
  Soon hurries me back to despair.

But the sea fowl is gone to her nest,
  The beast is laid down in his lair,
Even here is a season of rest,
  And I to my cabin repair.
There is mercy in every place,
  And mercy, encouraging thought!
Gives even affliction a grace,
  And reconciles man to his lot.

The Modern Patriot

Rebellion is my theme all day,
　　I only wish 'twould come
(As who knows but perhaps it may)
　　A little nearer home.

5　Yon roaring boys who rave and fight
　　On t'other side the Atlantic,
I always held them in the right,
　　But most so, when most frantic.

When lawless mobs insult the court,
10　　That man shall be my toast,
If breaking windows be the sport
　　Who bravely breaks the most.

But oh! for him my fancy culls
　　The choicest flowers she bears,
15　Who constitutionally pulls
　　Your house about your ears.

Such civil broils are my delight,
　　Though some folks can't endure 'em,
Who say the mob are mad outright,
20　　And that a rope must cure 'em.

A rope! I wish we patriots had
　　Such strings for all who need 'em –
What! hang a man for going mad?
　　Then farewell British freedom.

The Winter Nosegay

What nature, alas! has denied
    To the delicate growth of our isle,
Art has in a measure supplied,
    And winter is decked with a smile.
5 See Mary what beauties I bring
    From the shelter of that sunny shed,
Where the flowers have the charms of the spring,
    Though abroad they are frozen and dead.

'Tis a bower of Arcadian sweets,
10   Where Flora is still in her prime,
A fortress to which she retreats,
    From the cruel assaults of the clime.
While earth wears a mantle of snow,
    These pinks are as fresh and as gay,
15 As the fairest and sweetest that blow,
    On the beautiful bosom of May.

See how they have safely survived
    The frowns of a sky so severe,
Such Mary's true love that has lived
20   Through many a turbulent year.
The charms of the late blowing rose
    Seem graced with a livelier hue,
And the winter of sorrow best shows
    The truth of a friend, such as you.

Boadicea, an Ode

When the British warrior queen,
    Bleeding from the Roman rods,
Sought with an indignant mien,
    Counsel of her country's gods,

5   Sage beneath a spreading oak
           Sat the druid, hoary chief,
       Every burning word he spoke,
           Full of rage and full of grief.

       'Princess! if our aged eyes
10   Weep upon thy matchless wrongs,
       'Tis because resentment ties
           All the terrors of our tongues.

       'Rome shall perish – write that word
           In the blood that she has spilt;
15   Perish hopeless and abhorred,
           Deep in ruin as in guilt.

       'Rome for empire far renowned,
           Tramples on a thousand states,
       Soon her pride shall kiss the ground –
20   Hark! the Gaul is at her gates.

       'Other Romans shall arise,
           Heedless of a soldier's name,
       Sounds, nor arms, shall win the prize,
           Harmony the path to fame.

25   'Then the progeny that springs
           From the forests of our land,
       Armed with thunder, clad with wings,
           Shall a wider world command.

       'Regions Caesar never knew,
30   Thy posterity shall sway,
       Where his eagles never flew,
           None invincible as they.'

       Such the bard's prophetic words,
           Pregnant with celestial fire,
35   Bending as he swept the chords
           Of his sweet but awful lyre.

She with all a monarch's pride,
    Felt them in her bosom glow,
Rushed to battle, fought and died,
40   Dying, hurled them at the foe.

'Ruffians, pitiless as proud,
    Heaven awards the vengeance due,
Empire is on us bestowed,
    Shame and ruin wait for you.'

The Poet, the Oyster, and Sensitive Plant

An oyster cast upon the shore
Was heard, though never heard before;
Complaining in a speech well worded,
And worthy thus to be recorded:
5   'Ah hapless wretch! condemned to dwell
For ever in my native shell,
Ordained to move when others please,
Not for my own content or ease,
But tossed and buffeted about,
10 Now *in* the water, and now *out*.
'Twere better to be born a stone
Of ruder shape and feeling none,
Than with a tenderness like mine,
And sensibilities so fine;
15 I envy that unfeeling shrub
Fast-rooted against every rub.'
The plant he meant grew not far off,
And felt the sneer with scorn enough,
Was hurt, disgusted, mortified,
20 And with asperity replied.
    When, cry the botanists, and stare,
Did plants called sensitive grow there?
No matter when – a poet's muse is
To make them grow just where she chooses.

25   'You shapeless nothing in a dish,
  You that are but almost a fish,
  I scorn your coarse insinuation,
  And have most plentiful occasion
  To wish myself the rock I view,
30 Or such another dolt as you.
  For many a grave and learned clerk,
  And many a gay unlettered spark,
  With curious touch examines me,
  If I can feel as well as he;
35 And when I bend, retire and shrink,
  Says, "Well – 'tis more than one would think" –
  Thus life is spent, oh fie upon't!
  In being touched, and crying, "Don't".'
   A poet in his evening walk,
40 O'erheard and checked this idle talk.
  'And your fine sense,' he said, 'and yours,
  Whatever evil it endures,
  Deserves not, if so soon offended,
  Much to be pitied or commended.
45 Disputes though short, are far too long,
  Where both alike are in the wrong;
  Your feelings in their full amount,
  Are all upon your own account.
   'You in your grotto-work enclosed
50 Complain of being thus exposed,
  Yet nothing feel in that rough coat,
  Save when the knife is at your throat,
  Wherever driven by wind or tide,
  Exempt from every ill beside.
55   'And as for you, my Lady Squeamish,
  Who reckon every touch a blemish,
  If all the plants that can be found
  Embellishing the scene around,
  Should droop and wither where they grow,
60 You would not feel at all, not you.
  The noblest minds their virtue prove
  By pity, sympathy, and love,

These, these are feelings truly fine,
And prove their owner half divine.'
65   His censure reached them as he dealt it,
And each by shrinking showed he felt it.

To the Rev. William Cawthorne Unwin

Unwin, I should but ill repay
    The kindness of a friend,
Whose worth deserves as warm a lay
    As ever friendship penned,
5 Thy name omitted in a page,
That would reclaim a vicious age.

An union formed, as mine with thee,
    Not rashly or in sport,
May be as fervent in degree,
10   And faithful in its sort,
And may as rich in comfort prove,
As that of true fraternal love.

The bud inserted in the rind,
    The bud of peach or rose,
15 Adorns, though differing in its kind,
    The stock whereon it grows
With flower as sweet or fruit as fair,
As if produced by nature there.

Not rich, I render what I may,
20   I seize thy name in haste,
And place it in this first assay,
    Lest this should prove the last.
'Tis where it should be, in a plan
That holds in view the good of man.

25   The poet's lyre, to fix his fame,
            Should be the poet's heart,
        Affection lights a brighter flame
            Than ever blazed by art.
    No muses on these lines attend,
    I sink the poet in the friend.

On the Loss of the Royal George

BY DESIRE OF LADY AUSTEN WHO WANTED WORDS TO
THE MARCH IN SCIPIO

    Toll for the brave – the brave that are no more –
    All sunk beneath the wave, fast by their native shore –
    Eight hundred of the brave, whose courage well was tried,
    Had made the vessel heel and laid her on her side;
5   A land-breeze shook the shrouds, and she was overset,
    Down went the Royal George, with all her crew complete.

    Toll for the brave – brave Kempenfelt is gone,
    His last sea-fight is fought – his work of glory done –
    It was not in the battle – no tempest gave the shock,
10 She sprang no fatal leak, she ran upon no rock;
    His sword was in the sheath, his fingers held the pen,
    When Kempenfelt went down, with twice four hundred men.

    Weigh the vessel up, once dreaded by our foes,
    And mingle with your cup the tears that England owes;
15 Her timbers yet are sound, and she may float again,
    Full charged with England's thunder, and plough the
            distant main –
    But Kempenfelt is gone, his victories are o'er,
    And he and his eight hundred must plough the wave no
            more.

Epitaph on a Hare

Here lies, whom hound did ne'er pursue
　　　Nor swifter greyhound follow,
Whose foot ne'er tainted morning dew
　　　Nor ear heard huntsman's hallo,

5　Old Tiney, surliest of his kind,
　　　Who, nursed with tender care,
And to domestic bounds confined,
　　　Was still a wild Jack-hare.

Though duly from my hand he took
10　　　His pittance every night,
He did it with a jealous look,
　　　And, when he could, would bite.

His diet was of wheaten bread
　　　And milk, and oats, and straw,
15　Thistles, or lettuces instead,
　　　With sand to scour his maw.

On twigs of hawthorn he regaled,
　　　On pippins' russet peel,
And, when his juicy salads failed,
20　　　Sliced carrot pleased him well.

A Turkey carpet was his lawn
　　　Whereon he loved to bound,
To skip and gambol like a fawn,
　　　And swing his rump around.

25　His frisking was at evening hours,
　　　For then he lost his fear,
But most before approaching showers
　　　Or when a storm drew near.

Eight years and five round-rolling moons
30   He thus saw steal away,
Dozing out all his idle noons,
        And every night at play.

I kept him for his humour's sake,
        For he would oft beguile
35 My heart of thoughts that made it ache,
        And force me to a smile.

But now, beneath this walnut-shade
        He finds his long last home,
And waits in snug concealment laid
40   Till gentler Puss shall come.

He, still more aged, feels the shocks
        From which no care can save,
And, partner once of Tiney's box,
        Must soon partake his grave.

The Poplar-Field

The poplars are felled, farewell to the shade
And the whispering sound of the cool colonnade,
The winds play no longer and sing in the leaves,
Nor Ouse on his bosom their image receives.

5 Twelve years have elapsed since I first took a view
Of my favourite field and the bank where they grew,
And now in the grass behold they are laid,
And the tree is my seat that once lent me a shade.

The blackbird has fled to another retreat
10 Where the hazels afford him a screen from the heat,
And the scene where his melody charmed me before,
Resounds with his sweet-flowing ditty no more.

My fugitive years are all hasting away,
And I must e're long lie as lowly as they,
15 With a turf on my breast and a stone at my head
E're another such grove shall arise in its stead.

'Tis a sight to engage me, if any thing can,
To muse on the perishing pleasures of man;
Though his life be a dream, his enjoyments, I see,
20 Have a being less durable even than he.

To the Immortal Memory of the Halibut
on which I Dined this Day

Where hast thou floated, in what seas pursued
Thy pastime? When wast thou an egg new-spawned,
Lost in the immensity of ocean's waste?
Roar as they might, the overbearing winds
5 That rocked the deep, thy cradle, thou wast safe,
And in thy minikin and embryo state,
Attached to the firm leaf of some salt weed,
Didst outlive tempests, such as wrung and racked
The joints of many a stout and gallant bark,
10 And whelmed them in the unexplored abyss.
Indebted to no magnet and no chart,
Nor under guidance of the polar fire,
Thou wast a voyager on many coasts,
Grazing at large in meadows submarine,
15 Where flat Batavia just emerging peeps
Above the brine, where Caledonia's rocks
Beat back the surge, and where Hibernia shoots
Her wondrous causeway far into the main.
Wherever thou hast fed, thou little thought'st,
20 And I not more, that I should feed on thee.
Peace therefore and good health and much good fish
To him who sent thee, and success, as oft
As it descends into the billowy gulph,
To the same drag that caught thee. Fare thee well,

25   Thy lot thy brethren of the slimy fin
      Would envy, could they know that thou wast doomed
      To feed a bard and to be praised in verse.

from *Tirocinium: or, a Review of Schools*

I
      Would you your son should be a sot or dunce,
      Lascivious, headstrong, or all these at once;
      That, in good time, the stripling's finished taste
      For loose expense and fashionable waste
205   Should prove your ruin and his own at last;
      Train him in public with a mob of boys,
      Childish in mischief only and in noise,
      Else of a mannish growth, and five in ten
      In infidelity and lewdness, men.
210   There shall he learn, e're sixteen winters old,
      That authors are most useful pawned or sold;
      That pedantry is all that schools impart,
      But taverns teach the knowledge of the heart;
      There waiter Dick with Bacchanalian lays
215   Shall win his heart and have his drunken praise,
      His counsellor and bosom-friend shall prove,
      And some street-pacing harlot his first love.
      Schools, unless discipline were doubly strong,
      Detain their adolescent charge too long.
220   The management of tiros of eighteen
      Is difficult, their punishment obscene.
      The stout tall Captain, whose superior size
      The minor heroes view with envious eyes,
      Becomes their pattern, upon whom they fix
225   Their whole attention, and ape all his tricks.
      His pride, that scorns t'obey or to submit,
      With them is courage, his effrontery wit.
      His wild excursions, window-breaking feats,
      Robbery of gardens, quarrels in the streets,

230 His hair-breadth 'scapes, and all his daring schemes,
Transport them, and are made their favourite themes.
In little bosoms such achievements strike
A kindred spark; they burn to do the like.
Thus, half-accomplished e're he yet begin
235 To show the peeping down upon his chin,
And as maturity of years comes on,
Made just the adept that you designed your son;
To ensure the perseverance of his course,
And give your monstrous project all its force,
240 Send him to college. If he there be tamed,
Or in one article of vice reclaimed,
Where no regard of ordinances is shown
Or looked for now, the fault must be his own.
Some sneaking virtue lurks in him no doubt,
245 Where neither strumpets' charms, nor drinking-bout,
Nor gambling practices can find it out.
Such youths of spirit, and that spirit too,
Ye nurseries of our boys, we owe to you!
Though from ourselves the mischief more proceeds,
250 For public schools 'tis public folly feeds.

II
Be it a weakness, it deserves some praise,
We love the play-place of our early days.
The scene is touching, and the heart is stone
That feels not at that sight, and feels at none.
300 The wall on which we tried our graving skill,
The very name we carved subsisting still;
The bench on which we sat while deep employed,
Though mangled, hacked, and hewed, not yet destroyed,
The little ones, unbuttoned, glowing hot,
305 Playing our games, and on the very spot,
As happy as we once, to kneel and draw
The chalky ring, and knuckle down at taw,
To pitch the ball into the grounded hat,
Or drive it devious with a dextrous pat;
310 The pleasing spectacle at once excites
Such recollection of our own delights,

That viewing it, we seem almost to obtain
Our innocent sweet simple years again.
This fond attachment to the well-known place
315 Whence first we started into life's long race,
Maintains its hold with such unfailing sway,
We feel it even in age, and at our latest day.
Hark! how the sire of chits, whose future share
Of classic food begins to be his care,
320 With his own likeness placed on either knee,
Indulges all a father's heart-felt glee,
And tells them as he strokes their silver locks,
That they must soon learn Latin, and to box;
Then turning, he regales his listening wife
325 With all the adventures of his early life:
His skill in coachmanship or driving chaise,
In bilking tavern bills and spouting plays,
What shifts he used, detected in a scrape,
How he was flogged, or had the luck to escape;
330 What sums he lost at play, and how he sold
Watch, seals, and all, till all his pranks are told.
Retracing thus his *frolics*, ('tis a name
That palliates deeds of folly and of shame)
He gives the local bias all its sway,
335 Resolves that where he played his sons shall play,
And destines their bright genius to be shown
Just in the scene where he displayed his own.
The meek and bashful boy will soon be taught
To be as bold and forward as he ought,
340 The rude will scuffle through with ease enough,
Great schools suit best the sturdy and the rough.
Ah, happy designation, prudent choice,
The event is sure; expect it and rejoice!
Soon see your wish fulfilled in either child,
345 The pert made perter, and the tame made wild.

The Winter Evening
(Book IV of *The Task*)

Hark! 'tis the twanging horn! o'er yonder bridge
That with its wearisome but needful length
Bestrides the wintry flood, in which the moon
Sees her unwrinkled face reflected bright,
5   He comes, the herald of a noisy world,
With spattered boots, strapped waist, and frozen locks,
News from all nations lumbering at his back.
True to his charge the close-packed load behind,
Yet careless what he brings, his one concern
10   Is to conduct it to the destined inn,
And having dropped the expected bag – pass on.
He whistles as he goes, light-hearted wretch,
Cold and yet cheerful: messenger of grief
Perhaps to thousands, and of joy to some,
15   To him indifferent whether grief or joy.
Houses in ashes, and the fall of stocks,
Births, deaths, and marriages, epistles wet
With tears that trickled down the writer's cheeks
Fast as the periods from his fluent quill,

20   Or charged with amorous sighs of absent swains
       Or nymphs responsive, equally affect
       His horse and him, unconscious of them all.
       But oh the important budget! ushered in
       With such heart-shaking music, who can say
25   What are its tidings? have our troops awaked?
       Or do they still, as if with opium drugged,
       Snore to the murmurs of the Atlantic wave?
       Is India free? and does she wear her plumed
       And jewelled turban with a smile of peace,
30   Or do we grind her still? the grand debate,
       The popular harangue, the tart reply,
       The logic and the wisdom and the wit
       And the loud laugh – I long to know them all;
       I burn to set the imprisoned wranglers free,
35   And give them voice and utterance once again.
           Now stir the fire, and close the shutters fast,
       Let fall the curtains, wheel the sofa round,
       And while the bubbling and loud-hissing urn
       Throws up a steamy column, and the cups
40   That cheer but not inebriate, wait on each,
       So let us welcome peaceful evening in.
       Not such his evening, who with shining face
       Sweats in the crowded theatre, and squeezed
       And bored with elbow-points through both his sides,
45   Out-scolds the ranting actor on the stage.
       Nor his, who patient stands till his feet throb
       And his head thumps, to feed upon the breath
       Of patriots bursting with heroic rage,
       Or placemen, all tranquillity and smiles.
50   This folio of four pages, happy work!
       Which not even critics criticise, that holds
       Inquisitive attention while I read
       Fast bound in chains of silence, which the fair,
       Though eloquent themselves, yet fear to break,
55   What is it but a map of busy life,
       Its fluctuations and its vast concerns?
       Here runs the mountainous and craggy ridge
       That tempts ambition. On the summit, see,

The seals of office glitter in his eyes;
60   He climbs, he pants, he grasps them. At his heels,
Close at his heels a demagogue ascends,
And with a dextrous jerk soon twists him down
And wins them, but to lose them in his turn.
Here rills of oily eloquence in soft
65   Meanders lubricate the course they take;
The modest speaker is ashamed and grieved
T'engross a moment's notice, and yet begs,
Begs a propitious ear for his poor thoughts,
However trivial all that he conceives.
70   Sweet bashfulness! it claims at least this praise,
The dearth of information and good sense
That it foretells us always comes to pass.
Cataracts of declamation thunder here,
There forests of no-meaning spread the page
75   In which all comprehension wanders lost;
While fields of pleasantry amuse us there,
With merry descants on a nation's woes.
The rest appears a wilderness of strange
But gay confusion, roses for the cheeks
80   And lilies for the brows of faded age,
Teeth for the toothless, ringlets for the bald,
Heaven, earth, and ocean plundered of their sweets,
Nectareous essences, Olympian dews,
Sermons and city feasts and favourite airs,
85   Ethereal journeys, submarine exploits,
And Katterfelto with his hair on end
At his own wonders, wondering for his bread.
      'Tis pleasant through the loop-holes of retreat
To peep at such a world. To see the stir
90   Of the great Babel and not feel the crowd.
To hear the roar she sends through all her gates
At a safe distance, where the dying sound
Falls a soft murmur on the uninjured ear.
Thus sitting and surveying thus at ease
95   The globe and its concerns, I seem advanced
To some secure and more than mortal height,
That liberates and exempts me from them all.

It turns submitted to my view, turns round
With all its generations; I behold
100   The tumult and am still. The sound of war
Has lost its terrors e're it reaches me,
Grieves but alarms me not. I mourn the pride
And avarice that makes man a wolf to man,
Hear the faint echo of those brazen throats
105   By which he speaks the language of his heart,
And sigh, but never tremble at the sound.
He travels and expatiates, as the bee
From flower to flower, so he from land to land;
The manners, customs, policy of all
110   Pay contribution to the store he gleans,
He sucks intelligence in every clime,
And spreads the honey of his deep research
At his return, a rich repast for me.
He travels and I too. I tread his deck,
115   Ascend his topmast, through his peering eyes
Discover countries, with a kindred heart
Suffer his woes and share in his escapes,
While fancy, like the finger of a clock,
Runs the great circuit, and is still at home.

120   Oh Winter! ruler of the inverted year,
Thy scattered hair with sleet like ashes filled,
Thy breath congealed upon thy lips, thy cheeks
Fringed with a beard made white with other snows
Than those of age; thy forehead wrapped in clouds,
125   A leafless branch thy sceptre, and thy throne
A sliding car indebted to no wheels,
But urged by storms along its slippery way;
I love thee, all unlovely as thou seem'st,
And dreaded as thou art. Thou hold'st the sun
130   A prisoner in the yet undawning East,
Shortening his journey between morn and noon,
And hurrying him impatient of his stay
Down to the rosy West. But kindly still
Compensating his loss with added hours
135   Of social converse and instructive ease,
And gathering at short notice in one group

The family dispersed, and fixing thought
Not less dispersed by day-light and its cares.
I crown thee King of intimate delights,
140   Fireside enjoyments, home-born happiness,
And all the comforts that the lowly roof
Of undisturbed retirement, and the hours
Of long uninterrupted evening, know.
No rattling wheels stop short before these gates,
145   No powdered pert proficient in the art
Of sounding an alarm, assaults these doors
Till the street rings. No stationary steeds
Cough their own knell, while heedless of the sound
The silent circle fan themselves, and quake.
150   But here the needle plies its busy task,
The pattern grows, the well-depicted flower
Wrought patiently into the snowy lawn
Unfolds its bosom, buds and leaves and sprigs
And curling tendrils, gracefully disposed,
155   Follow the nimble fingers of the fair,
A wreath that cannot fade, of flowers that blow
With most success when all besides decay.
The poet's or historian's page, by one
Made vocal for the amusement of the rest;
160   The sprightly lyre, whose treasure of sweet sounds
The touch from many a trembling chord shakes out;
And the clear voice symphonious, yet distinct,
And in the charming strife triumphant still,
Beguile the night, and set a keener edge
165   On female industry; the threaded steel
Flies swiftly, and unfelt the task proceeds.
The volume closed, the customary rites
Of the last meal commence. A Roman meal;
Such as the mistress of the world once found
170   Delicious, when her patriots of high note,
Perhaps by moonlight, at their humble doors,
And under an old oak's domestic shade
Enjoyed, spare feast! a radish and an egg.
Discourse ensues, not trivial, yet not dull,
175   Nor such as with a frown forbids the play

Of fancy, or proscribes the sound of mirth.
Nor do we madly, like an impious world,
Who deem religion frenzy, and the God
That made them an intruder on their joys,
180 Start at his awful name, or deem his praise
A jarring note. Themes of a graver tone
Exciting oft our gratitude and love,
While we retrace with memory's pointing wand
That calls the past to our exact review,
185 The dangers we have 'scaped, the broken snare,
The disappointed foe, deliverance found
Unlooked for, life preserved and peace restored,
Fruits of omnipotent eternal love.
Oh evenings worthy of the Gods! exclaimed
190 The Sabine bard. Oh evenings, I reply,
More to be prized and coveted than yours,
As more illumined and with nobler truths,
That I and mine and those we love, enjoy.
       Is winter hideous in a garb like this?
195 Needs he the tragic fur, the smoke of lamps,
The pent-up breath of an unsavoury throng
To thaw him into feeling, or the smart
And snappish dialogue that flippant wits
Call comedy, to prompt him with a smile?
200 The self-complacent actor when he views
(Stealing a sidelong glance at a full house)
The slope of faces from the floor to the roof,
(As if one master-spring controlled them all)
Relaxed into an universal grin,
205 Sees not a countenance there that speaks a joy
Half so refined or so sincere as ours.
Cards were superfluous here, with all the tricks
That idleness has ever yet contrived
To fill the void of an unfurnished brain,
210 To palliate dullness and give time a shove.
Time as he passes us, has a dove's wing,
Unsoiled and swift and of a silken sound.
But the world's time is time in masquerade.
Theirs, should I paint him, has his pinions fledged

215 With motley plumes, and where the peacock shows
      His azure eyes, is tinctured black and red
      With spots quadrangular of diamond form,
      Ensanguined hearts, clubs typical of strife,
      And spades, the emblem of untimely graves.
220 What should be and what was an hour-glass once
      Becomes a dice-box, and a billiard mast
      Well does the work of his destructive scythe.
      Thus decked he charms a world whom fashion blinds
      To his true worth, most pleased when idle most,
225 Whose only happy are their wasted hours.
      Even misses, at whose age their mothers wore
      The back-string and the bib, assume the dress
      Of womanhood, sit pupils in the school
      Of card-devoted time, and night by night
230 Placed at some vacant corner of the board,
      Learn every trick, and soon play all the game.
      But truce with censure. Roving as I rove,
      Where shall I find an end, or how proceed?
      As he that travels far oft turns aside
235 To view some rugged rock or mouldering tower,
      Which seen delights him not; then coming home,
      Describes and prints it, that the world may know
      How far he went for what was nothing worth;
      So I with brush in hand and pallet spread
240 With colours mixed for a far different use,
      Paint cards and dolls, and every idle thing
      That fancy finds in her excursive flights.
          Come Evening once again, season of peace,
      Return sweet Evening, and continue long!
245 Methinks I see thee in the streaky west,
      With matron-step slow-moving, while the night
      Treads on thy sweeping train; one hand employed
      In letting fall the curtain of repose
      On bird and beast, the other charged for man
250 With sweet oblivion of the cares of day;
      Not sumptuously adorned, nor needing aid
      Like homely featured night, of clustering gems,
      A star or two just twinkling on thy brow

Suffices thee; save that the moon is thine
255 No less than hers, not worn indeed on high
With ostentatious pageantry, but set
With modest grandeur in thy purple zone,
Resplendent less, but of an ampler round.
Come then, and thou shalt find thy votary calm
260 Or make me so. Composure is thy gift.
And whether I devote thy gentle hours
To books, to music, or the poet's toil,
To weaving nets for bird-alluring fruit;
Or twining silken threads round ivory reels
265 When they command whom man was born to please,
I slight thee not, but make thee welcome still.
      Just when our drawing-rooms begin to blaze
With lights by clear reflection multiplied
From many a mirror, in which he of Gath,
270 Goliah, might have seen his giant bulk
Whole without stooping, towering crest and all,
My pleasures too begin. But me perhaps
The glowing hearth may satisfy awhile
With faint illumination that uplifts
275 The shadow to the ceiling, there by fits
Dancing uncouthly to the quivering flame.
Not undelightful is an hour to me
So spent in parlour twilight; such a gloom
Suits well the thoughtful or unthinking mind,
280 The mind contemplative, with some new theme
Pregnant, or indisposed alike to all.
Laugh ye, who boast your more mercurial powers,
That never feel a stupor, know no pause
Nor need one. I am conscious, and confess
285 Fearless, a soul that does not always think.
Me oft has fancy ludicrous and wild
Soothed with a waking dream of houses, towers,
Trees, churches, and strange visages expressed
In the red cinders, while with poring eye
290 I gazed, myself creating what I saw.
Nor less amused have I quiescent watched
The sooty films that play upon the bars,

Pendulous, and foreboding, in the view
Of superstition prophesying still
295 Though still deceived, some stranger's near approach.
'Tis thus the understanding takes repose
In indolent vacuity of thought,
And sleeps and is refreshed. Meanwhile the face
Conceals the mood lethargic with a mask
300 Of deep deliberation, as the man
Were tasked to his full strength, absorbed and lost.
Thus oft reclined at ease, I lose an hour
At evening, till at length the freezing blast
That sweeps the bolted shutter, summons home
305 The recollected powers, and snapping short
The glassy threads with which the fancy weaves
Her brittle toys, restores me to myself.
How calm is my recess, and how the frost
Raging abroad, and the rough wind, endear
310 The silence and the warmth enjoyed within.
I saw the woods and fields at close of day
A variegated show; the meadows green
Though faded, and the lands where lately waved
The golden harvest, of a mellow brown,
315 Upturned so lately by the forceful share.
I saw far off the weedy fallows smile
With verdure not unprofitable, grazed
By flocks fast feeding and selecting each
His favourite herb; while all the leafless groves
320 That skirt the horizon wore a sable hue,
Scarce noticed in the kindred dusk of eve.
Tomorrow brings a change, a total change!
Which even now, though silently performed
And slowly, and by most unfelt, the face
325 Of universal nature undergoes.
Fast falls a fleecy shower. The downy flakes
Descending and with never-ceasing lapse
Softly alighting upon all below,
Assimilate all objects. Earth receives
330 Gladly the thickening mantle, and the green
And tender blade that feared the chilling blast,

Escapes unhurt beneath so warm a veil.
        In such a world, so thorny, and where none
Finds happiness unblighted, or if found,
335   Without some thistly sorrow at its side,
It seems the part of wisdom, and no sin
Against the law of love, to measure lots
With less distinguished than ourselves, that thus
We may with patience bear our moderate ills,
340   And sympathise with others, suffering more.
Ill fares the traveller now, and he that stalks
In ponderous boots beside his reeking team.
The wain goes heavily, impeded sore
By congregated loads adhering close
345   To the clogged wheels; and in its sluggish pace
Noiseless, appears a moving hill of snow.
The toiling steeds expand the nostril wide,
While every breath by respiration strong
Forced downward, is consolidated soon
350   Upon their jutting chests. He, formed to bear
The pelting brunt of the tempestuous night,
With half-shut eyes and puckered cheeks, and teeth
Presented bare against the storm, plods on.
One hand secures his hat, save when with both
355   He brandishes his pliant length of whip,
Resounding oft, and never heard in vain.
Oh happy! and in my account, denied
That sensibility of pain with which
Refinement is endued, thrice happy thou.
360   Thy frame robust and hardy, feels indeed
The piercing cold, but feels it unimpaired.
The learnèd finger never need explore
Thy vigorous pulse, and the unhealthful East,
That breathes the spleen, and searches every bone
365   Of the infirm, is wholesome air to thee.
Thy days roll on exempt from household care,
The waggon is thy wife; and the poor beasts
That drag the dull companion to and fro,
Thine helpless charge, dependent on thy care.
370   Ah treat them kindly! rude as thou appear'st

Yet show that thou hast mercy, which the great
With needless hurry whirled from place to place,
Humane as they would seem, not always show.
    Poor, yet industrious, modest, quiet, neat,
375 Such claim compassion in a night like this,
And have a friend in every feeling heart.
Warmed, while it lasts, by labour, all day long
They brave the season, and yet find at eve,
Ill clad and fed but sparely, time to cool.
380 The frugal housewife trembles when she lights
Her scanty stock of brush-wood, blazing clear
But dying soon, like all terrestrial joys.
The few small embers left she nurses well,
And while her infant race with outspread hands
385 And crowded knees sit cowering o'er the sparks,
Retires, content to quake, so they be warmed.
The man feels least, as more inured than she
To winter, and the current in his veins
More briskly moved by his severer toil;
390 Yet he too finds his own distress in theirs.
The taper soon extinguished, which I saw
Dangled along at the cold finger's end
Just when the day declined, and the brown loaf
Lodged on the shelf half-eaten without sauce
395 Of savoury cheese, or butter costlier still,
Sleep seems their only refuge. For, alas!
Where penury is felt the thought is chained,
And sweet colloquial pleasures are but few.
With all this thrift they thrive not. All the care
400 Ingenious parsimony takes but just
Saves the small inventory, bed and stool,
Skillet and old carved chest from public sale.
They live, and live without extorted alms
From grudging hands, but other boast have none
405 To soothe their honest pride that scorns to beg,
Nor comfort else, but in their mutual love.
I praise you much, ye meek and patient pair,
For ye are worthy; choosing rather far
A dry but independent crust, hard-earned

410   And eaten with a sigh, than to endure
      The rugged frowns and insolent rebuffs
      Of knaves in office, partial in the work
      Of distribution; liberal of their aid
      To clamorous importunity in rags,
415   But oft-times deaf to suppliants who would blush
      To wear a tattered garb however coarse,
      Whom famine cannot reconcile to filth;
      These ask with painful shyness, and refused
      Because deserving, silently retire.
420   But be ye of good courage. Time itself
      Shall much befriend you. Time shall give increase,
      And all your numerous progeny well-trained
      But helpless, in few years shall find their hands,
      And labour too. Meanwhile ye shall not want
425   What conscious of your virtues we can spare,
      Nor what a wealthier than ourselves may send,
      I mean the man, who when the distant poor
      Need help, denies them nothing but his name.
            But poverty with most who whimper forth
430   Their long complaints, is self-inflicted woe,
      The effect of laziness or sottish waste.
      Now goes the nightly thief prowling abroad
      For plunder; much solicitous how best
      He may compensate for a day of sloth,
435   By works of darkness and nocturnal wrong.
      Woe to the gardener's pale, the farmer's hedge,
      Plashed neatly, and secured with driven stakes
      Deep in the loamy bank. Uptorn by strength
      Resistless in so bad a cause, but lame
440   To better deeds, he bundles up the spoil,
      An ass's burthen, and when laden most
      And heaviest, light of foot steals fast away.
      Nor does the boarded hovel better guard
      The well-stacked pile of riven logs and roots
445   From his pernicious force. Nor will he leave
      Unwrenched the door however well secured,
      Where chanticleer amidst his harem sleeps
      In unsuspecting pomp. Twitched from the perch

He gives the princely bird with all his wives
450 To his voracious bag, struggling in vain,
And loudly wondering at the sudden change.
Nor this to feed his own. 'Twere some excuse
Did pity of their sufferings warp aside
His principle, and tempt him into sin
455 For their support, so destitute. But they
Neglected pine at home, themselves, as more
Exposed than others, with less scruple made
His victims, robbed of their defenceless all.
Cruel is all he does. 'Tis quenchless thirst
460 Of ruinous ebriety that prompts
His every action and imbrutes the man.
Oh for a law to noose the villain's neck
Who starves his own; who persecutes the blood
He gave them in his children's veins, and hates
465 And wrongs the woman he has sworn to love.
        Pass where we may, through city or through town,
Village or hamlet of this merry land,
Though lean and beggared, every twentieth pace
Conducts the unguarded nose to such a whiff
470 Of stale debauch forth-issuing from the sties
That law has licensed, as makes temperance reel.
There sit involved and lost in curling clouds
Of Indian fume, and guzzling deep, the boor,
The lackey and the groom. The craftsman there
475 Takes a Lethean leave of all his toil;
Smith, cobbler, joiner, he that plies the shears,
And he that kneads the dough; all loud alike,
All learnèd, and all drunk. The fiddle screams
Plaintive and piteous, as it wept and wailed
480 Its wasted tones and harmony unheard:
Fierce the dispute whate'er the theme. While she,
Fell Discord, arbitress of such debate,
Perched on the sign-post, holds with even hand
Her undecisive scales. In this she lays
485 A weight of ignorance, in that, of pride,
And smiles, delighted with the eternal poise.
Dire is the frequent curse and its twin sound

The cheek-distending oath, not to be praised
As ornamental, musical, polite,
490   Like those which modern senators employ,
Whose oath is rhetoric, and who swear for fame.
Behold the schools in which plebeian minds,
Once simple, are initiated in arts
Which some may practise with politer grace,
495   But none with readier skill! 'tis here they learn
The road that leads from competence and peace
To indigence and rapine; till at last
Society grown weary of the load,
Shakes her incumbered lap, and casts them out.
500   But censure profits little. Vain the attempt
To advertise in verse a public pest,
That like the filth with which the peasant feeds
His hungry acres, stinks and is of use.
The excise is fattened with the rich result
505   Of all this riot. And ten thousand casks
For ever dribbling out their base contents,
Touched by the Midas finger of the state,
Bleed gold for ministers to sport away.
Drink and be mad then. 'Tis your country bids.
510   Gloriously drunk obey the important call,
Her cause demands the assistance of your throats,
Ye all can swallow, and she asks no more.
         Would I had fallen upon those happier days
That poets celebrate. Those golden times
515   And those Arcadian scenes that Maro sings,
And Sidney, warbler of poetic prose.
Nymphs were Dianas then, and swains had hearts
That felt their virtues. Innocence, it seems,
From courts dismissed, found shelter in the groves.
520   The footsteps of simplicity impressed
Upon the yielding herbage (so they sing)
Then were not all effaced. Then, speech profane
And manners profligate were rarely found,
Observed as prodigies, and soon reclaimed.
525   Vain wish! those days were never. Airy dreams
Sat for the picture. And the poet's hand

Imparting substance to an empty shade,
Imposed a gay delirium for a truth.
Grant it:– I still must envy them an age
530 That favoured such a dream, in days like these
Impossible, when virtue is so scarce
That to suppose a scene where she presides,
Is tramontane, and stumbles all belief.
No. We are polished now. The rural lass
535 Whom once her virgin modesty and grace,
Her artless manners and her neat attire
So dignified, that she was hardly less
Than the fair shepherdess of old romance,
Is seen no more. The character is lost.
540 Her head adorned with lappets pinned aloft
And ribbands streaming gay, superbly raised,
And magnified beyond all human size,
Indebted to some smart wig-weaver's hand
For more than half the tresses it sustains;
545 Her elbows ruffled, and her tottering form
Ill propped upon French heels; she might be deemed
(But that the basket dangling on her arm
Interprets her more truly) of a rank
Too proud for dairy work or sale of eggs.
550 Expect her soon with foot-boy at her heels,
No longer blushing for her awkward load,
Her train and her umbrella all her care.
        The town has tinged the country. And the stain
Appears a spot upon a vestal's robe,
555 The worse for what it soils. The fashion runs
Down into scenes still rural, but alas!
Scenes rarely graced with rural manners now.
Time was when in the pastoral retreat
The unguarded door was safe. Men did not watch
560 To invade another's right, or guard their own.
Then sleep was undisturbed by fear, unscared
By drunken howlings; and the chilling tale
Of midnight murther was a wonder heard
With doubtful credit, told to frighten babes.
565 But farewell now to unsuspicious nights

And slumbers unalarmed. Now e're you sleep
See that your polished arms be primed with care,
And drop the night-bolt. Ruffians are abroad,
And the first larum of the cock's shrill throat
570   May prove a trumpet, summoning your ear
To horrid sounds of hostile feet within.
Even day-light has its dangers. And the walk
Through pathless wastes and woods, unconscious once
Of other tenants than melodious birds
575   Or harmless flocks, is hazardous and bold.
Lamented change! to which full many a cause
Inveterate, hopeless of a cure, conspires.
The course of human things from good to ill,
From ill to worse, is fatal, never fails.
580   Increase of power begets increase of wealth,
Wealth luxury, and luxury excess;
Excess, the scrofulous and itchy plague
That seizes first the opulent, descends
To the next rank contagious, and in time
585   Taints downward all the graduated scale
Of order, from the chariot to the plough.
The rich, and they that have an arm to check
The license of the lowest in degree,
Desert their office; and themselves intent
590   On pleasure, haunt the capital, and thus
To all the violence of lawless hands
Resign the scenes their presence might protect.
Authority herself not seldom sleeps,
Though resident, and witness of the wrong.
595   The plump convivial parson often bears
The magisterial sword in vain, and lays
His reverence and his worship both to rest
On the same cushion of habitual sloth.
Perhaps timidity restrains his arm;
600   When he should strike, he trembles, and sets free,
Himself enslaved by terror of the band,
The audacious convict whom he dares not bind.
Perhaps, though by profession ghostly pure,
He too may have his vice, and sometimes prove

605 Less dainty than becomes his grave outside
In lucrative concerns. Examine well
His milk-white hand. The palm is hardly clean –
But here and there an ugly smutch appears.
Foh! 'twas a bribe that left it. He has touched
610 Corruption. Whoso seeks an audit here
Propitious, pays his tribute, game or fish,
Wild-fowl or venison, and his errand speeds.
      But faster far and more than all the rest
A noble cause, which none who bears a spark
615 Of public virtue ever wished removed,
Works the deplored and mischievous effect.
'Tis universal soldiership has stabbed
The heart of merit in the meaner class.
Arms through the vanity and brainless rage
620 Of those that bear them in whatever cause,
Seem most at variance with all moral good,
And incompatible with serious thought.
The clown, the child of nature, without guile,
Blessed with an infant's ignorance of all
625 But his own simple pleasures, now and then
A wrestling match, a foot-race, or a fair,
Is ballotted, and trembles at the news.
Sheepish he doffs his hat, and mumbling swears
A Bible-oath to be whate'er they please,
630 To do he knows not what. The task performed
That instant he becomes the sergeant's care,
His pupil, and his torment, and his jest.
His awkward gait, his introverted toes,
Bent knees, round shoulders, and dejected looks,
635 Procure him many a curse. By slow degrees,
Unapt to learn and formed of stubborn stuff,
He yet by slow degrees puts off himself,
Grows conscious of a change, and likes it well.
He stands erect, his slouch becomes a walk,
640 He steps right onward, martial in his air,
His form and movement; is as smart above
As meal and larded locks can make him; wears
His hat or his plumed helmet with a grace,

And, his three years of heroship expired,
645 Returns indignant to the slighted plough.
He hates the field in which no fife or drum
Attends him, drives his cattle to a march,
And sighs for the smart comrades he has left.
'Twere well if his exterior change were all –
650 But with his clumsy port the wretch has lost
His ignorance and harmless manners too.
To swear, to game, to drink, to show at home
By lewdness, idleness, and sabbath-breach,
The great proficiency he made abroad,
655 To astonish and to grieve his gazing friends,
To break some maiden's and his mother's heart,
To be a pest where he was useful once,
Are his sole aim, and all his glory now.
        Man in society is like a flower
660 Blown in its native bed. 'Tis there alone
His faculties expanded in full bloom
Shine out, there only reach their proper use.
But man associated and leagued with man
By regal warrant, or self-joined by bond
665 For interest-sake, or swarming into clans
Beneath one head for purposes of war,
Like flowers selected from the rest, and bound
And bundled close to fill some crowded vase,
Fades rapidly, and by compression marred
670 Contracts defilement not to be endured.
Hence chartered boroughs are such public plagues,
And burghers, men immaculate perhaps
In all their private functions, once combined
Become a loathsome body, only fit
675 For dissolution, hurtful to the main.
Hence merchants, unimpeachable of sin
Against the charities of domestic life,
Incorporated, seem at once to lose
Their nature, and disclaiming all regard
680 For mercy and the common rights of man,
Build factories with blood, conducting trade
At the sword's point, and dying the white robe

Of innocent commercial justice red.
Hence too the field of glory, as the world
685 Misdeems it, dazzled by its bright array,
With all its majesty of thundering pomp,
Enchanting music and immortal wreaths,
Is but a school where thoughtlessness is taught
On principle, where foppery atones
690 For folly, gallantry for every vice.
        But slighted as it is, and by the great
Abandoned, and, which still I more regret,
Infected with the manners and the modes
It knew not once, the country wins me still.
695 I never framed a wish, or formed a plan
That flattered me with hopes of earthly bliss,
But there I laid the scene. There early strayed
My fancy, 'ere yet liberty of choice
Had found me, or the hope of being free.
700 My very dreams were rural, rural too
The first-born efforts of my youthful muse
Sportive, and jingling her poetic bells
E're yet her ear was mistress of their powers.
No bard could please me but whose lyre was tuned
705 To Nature's praises. Heroes and their feats
Fatigued me, never weary of the pipe
Of Tityrus, assembling as he sang
The rustic throng beneath his favourite beech.
Then Milton had indeed a poet's charms.
710 New to my taste, his Paradise surpassed
The struggling efforts of my boyish tongue
To speak its excellence; I danced for joy.
I marvelled much that at so ripe an age
As twice seven years, his beauties had then first
715 Engaged my wonder, and admiring still
And still admiring, with regret supposed
The joy half lost because not sooner found.
Thee too enamoured of the life I loved,
Pathetic in its praise, in its pursuit
720 Determined, and possessing it at last
With transports such as favoured lovers feel,

I studied, prized, and wished that I had known
Ingenious Cowley! and though now reclaimed
By modern lights from an erroneous taste,
725 I cannot but lament thy splendid wit
Entangled in the cobwebs of the schools,
I still revere thee, courtly though retired,
Though stretched at ease in Chertsey's silent bowers
Not unemployed, and finding rich amends
730 For a lost world in solitude and verse.
'Tis born with all. The love of Nature's works
Is an ingredient in the compound, man,
Infused at the creation of the kind.
And though the Almighty Maker has throughout
735 Discriminated each from each, by strokes
And touches of his hand with so much art
Diversified, that two were never found
Twins at all points – yet this obtains in all,
That all discern a beauty in his works
740 And all can taste them. Minds that have been formed
And tutored, with a relish more exact,
But none without some relish, none unmoved.
It is a flame that dies not even there
Where nothing feeds it: neither business, crowds,
745 Nor habits of luxurious city-life,
Whatever else they smother of true worth
In human bosoms, quench it or abate.
The villas with which London stands begirt
Like a swarth Indian with his belt of beads,
750 Prove it. A breath of unadulterate air,
The glimpse of a green pasture, how they cheer
The citizen and brace his languid frame!
Even in the stifling bosom of the town,
A garden in which nothing thrives has charms
755 That soothe the rich possessor; much consoled
That here and there some sprigs of mournful mint,
Of nightshade or valerian grace the well
He cultivates. These serve him with a hint
That Nature lives, that sight-refreshing green
760 Is still the livery she delights to wear,

Though sickly samples of the exuberant whole.
What are the casements lined with creeping herbs,
The prouder sashes fronted with a range
Of orange, myrtle, or the fragrant weed,
765 The Frenchman's ¹darling? are they not all proofs
That man immured in cities, still retains
His inborn inextinguishable thirst
Of rural scenes, compensating his loss
By supplemental shifts, the best he may?
770 The most unfurnished with the means of life,
And they that never pass their brick-wall bounds
To range the fields and treat their lungs with air,
Yet feel the burning instinct: over-head
Suspend their crazy boxes planted thick
775 And watered duly. There the pitcher stands
A fragment, and the spoutless tea-pot there,
Sad witnesses how close-pent man regrets
The country, with what ardour he contrives
A peep at Nature, when he can no more.
780   Hail therefore patroness of health and ease
And contemplation, heart-consoling joys
And harmless pleasures in the thronged abode
Of multitudes unknown, hail rural life!
Address himself who will to the pursuit
785 Of honours or emolument or fame,
I shall not add myself to such a chase,
Thwart his attempts, or envy his success.
Some must be great. Great offices will have
Great talents. And God gives to every man
790 The virtue, temper, understanding, taste,
That lifts him into life, and lets him fall
Just in the niche he was ordained to fill.
To the deliverer of an injured land
He gives a tongue to enlarge upon, a heart
795 To feel, and courage to redress her wrongs;
To monarchs dignity, to judges sense,
To artists ingenuity and skill;

1. Mignonette.

To me an unambitious mind, content
In the low vale of life, that early felt
800 A wish for ease and leisure, and e're long
Found here that leisure and that ease I wished.

Verses Subjoined to the Bill of Mortality for the Town of Northampton, 1787

Pallida Mors aequo pulsat pede pauperum tabernas Regumque turres
Pale Death with equal foot strikes wide the door
Of royal halls and hovels of the poor.

While thirteen moons saw smoothly run
    The Nene's barge-laden wave,
All these, life's rambling journey done,
    Have found their home, the grave.

5   Was man (frail always) made more frail
    Than in foregoing years?
Did Famine, or did Plague prevail
    That so much Death appears?

No: these were vigorous as their sires,
10   Nor Plague nor Famine came;
This annual tribute Death requires
    And never waives his claim.

Like crowded forest-trees we stand,
    And some are marked to fall;
15 The axe will smite at God's command,
    And soon shall smite us all.

Green as the bay-tree ever green
    With its new foliage on,
The gay, the thoughtless I have seen,
20   I passed – and they were gone.

Read ye that run the awful truth
    With which I charge my page,
A worm is in the bud of youth,
    And at the root of age.

25   No present health can health insure
    For yet an hour to come,
No medicine, though it often cure,
    Can always baulk the tomb.

And oh! that (humble as my lot
30   And scorned as is my strain)
These truths, though known, too much forgot
    I may not teach in vain.

So prays your clerk with all his heart,
    And e're he quits the pen
35   Begs you for once to take his part,
    And answer all – Amen.

Pity for Poor Africans

– Video meliora, proboque
Deteriora sequor.
My mind far better things approves,
My heart far worse, in practice, loves.

'I own I am shocked at this traffic of slaves,
And fear those who buy them and sell them are knaves;
What I hear of their hardships, their tortures and groans,
Is almost enough to draw pity from stones.

5   'I pity them greatly, but I must be mum;
For how could we do without sugar and rum?
Especially sugar, so needful we see;
What? give up our desserts, our coffee, and tea?

'Besides, if we do, the French, Dutch, and Danes
10 Will heartily thank us, no doubt, for our pains;
If *we* do not buy the poor creatures *they* will,
And tortures and groans will be multiplied still.

'If foreigners likewise would give up the trade,
Much more in behalf of your wish might be said;
15 But while they get riches by purchasing blacks,
Pray tell me, why we may not also go snacks?'

'Your scruples and arguments bring to my mind
A story so pat, you may think it was coined,
On purpose to answer you, out of my mint;
20 But I can assure you I saw it in print.

'A youngster at school, more sedate than the rest,
Had once his integrity put to the test:
His comrades had plotted an orchard to rob,
And asked him to go and assist in the job.

25 'He was shocked, sir, like you, and answered – "Oh, no!
What! rob our good neighbour? – I pray you, don't go:
Besides, the man's poor, and his orchard's his bread;
Then think of his children, for they must be fed."

' "You talk very fine, and you look very grave,
30 But apples we want, and apples we'll have;
If you will go with us, we'll give you a share;
If not, you shall have neither apple or pear."

'They ceased, and Tom pondered, "I see they will go:
Poor man! what a pity to injure him so!
35 Poor man! I would save him his fruit, if I could,
But staying behind them will do him no good.

"If the matter depended alone upon me,
His apples might hang till they dropped from the tree;
But, since they will have them, I think I'll go too;
40 He'll lose none by me, though I get a few."

'His scruples thus silenced, Tom felt more at ease,
And went with his comrades the apples to seize;
He blamed and protested, but joined in the plan;
He shared in the plunder, but pitied the man.'

On the Receipt of my Mother's Picture out of Norfolk

THE GIFT OF MY COUSIN ANN BODHAM

Oh that those lips had language! Life has passed
With me but roughly since I heard thee last.
Those lips are thine – thy own sweet smiles I see –
The same that oft in childhood solaced me –
5   Voice only fails, else, how distinct they say –
Grieve not, my child, chase all thy fears away!
The meek intelligence of those dear eyes
(Blessed be the art that can immortalise,
The art that baffled Time's tyrannic claim
10   To quench it) here shines on me still the same.
     Faithful remembrancer of one so dear,
Oh welcome guest, though unexpected, here!
Who bidd'st me honour, with an artless song
Affectionate, a mother lost so long,
15   I will obey, not willingly alone
But gladly, as the precept were her own;
And while that face renews my filial grief
Fancy shall weave a charm for my relief,
Shall steep me in Elysian reverie,
20   A momentary dream, that thou art she.
     My mother! when I learned that thou wast dead
Say, wast thou conscious of the tears I shed?
Hovered thy spirit o'er thy sorrowing son,
Wretch even then, life's journey just begun?
25   Perhaps thou gav'st me, though unfelt, a kiss,
Perhaps a tear, if souls can weep in bliss –
Ah that maternal smile – it answers – yes.
I heard the bell tolled on thy burial day,

I saw the hearse that bore thee slow away,
30   And, turning from my nursery window, drew
A long long sigh, and wept a last adieu!
But was it such? It was – where thou art gone
Adieus and farewells are a sound unknown;
May I but meet thee on that peaceful shore
35   The parting word shall pass my lips no more.
Thy maidens grieved themselves at my concern,
Oft gave me promise of thy quick return;
What ardently I wished I long believed,
And, disappointed still, was still deceived,
40   By expectation every day beguiled,
Dupe of tomorrow even from a child.
Thus many a sad tomorrow came and went,
Till all my stock of infant sorrow spent
I learned at last submission to my lot,
45   But though I less deplored thee, ne'er forgot.
     Where once we dwelt, our name is heard no more;
Children, not thine, have trod my nursery floor;
And where the gardener Robin day by day
Drew me to school along the public way
50   Delighted with my bauble coach, and wrapped
In scarlet mantle warm and velvet-capped,
'Tis now become a history little known
That once we called the Pastoral house our own.
Short-lived possession! But the record fair
55   That memory keeps of all thy kindness there
Still outlives many a storm that has effaced
A thousand other themes less deeply traced.
Thy nightly visits to my chamber made
That thou might'st know me safe and warmly laid,
60   Thy morning bounties e'er I left my home,
The biscuit or confectionary plum,
The fragrant waters on my cheeks bestowed
By thy own hand, till fresh they shone and glowed,
All this, and more endearing still than all,
65   Thy constant flow of love that knew no fall,
Ne'er roughened by those cataracts and breaks
That humour interposed too often makes,

All this, still legible in memory's page
And still to be so to my latest age
70   Adds joy to duty, makes me glad to pay
Such honour to thee as my numbers may,
Perhaps a frail memorial, but sincere,
Not scorned in heaven, though little noticed here.
    Could Time, his flight reversed, restore the hours
75   When playing with thy vesture's tissued flowers,
The violet, the pink and jessamine,
I pricked them into paper with a pin,
(And thou wast happier than myself, the while,
Wouldst softly speak, and stroke my head and smile);
80   Could those few pleasant days again appear,
Might one wish bring them, would I wish them here?
I would not trust my heart, the dear delight
Seems so to be desired, perhaps I might –
But no – what here we call our life is such,
85   So little to be loved, and thou so much,
That I should ill requite thee to constrain
Thy unbound spirit into bonds again.
    Thou, as a gallant bark from Albion's coast
(The storms all weathered and the ocean crossed)
90   Shoots into port at some well-havened isle
Where spices breathe and brighter seasons smile,
There sits quiescent on the floods that show
Her beauteous form reflected clear below,
While airs, impregnated with incense, play
95   Around her, fanning light her streamers gay –
So thou, with sails how swift! hast reached the shore
'Where tempests never beat nor billows roar,'[1]
And thy loved consort on the dangerous tide
Of life, long since has anchored at thy side.
100   But me, scarce hoping to attain that rest,
Always from port withheld, always distressed,
Me howling blasts drive devious, tempest-tossed,
Sails ripped, seams opening wide and compass lost,

---

1. Garth [*The Dispensary*, III. 225–7].

And day by day some current's thwarting force
105   Sets me more distant from a prosperous course.
Yet oh the thought that thou art safe, and he!
That thought is joy, arrive what may to me.
My boast is, not that I deduce my birth
From loins enthroned and rulers of the earth,
110   But higher far my proud pretensions rise,
The son of parents passed into the skies.
       And now farewell – Time, unrevoked, has run
His wonted course, yet what I wished is done,
By Contemplation's help not sought in vain
115   I seem t'have lived my childhood o'er again,
To have renewed the joys that once were mine
Without the sin of violating thine;
And while the wings of Fancy still are free,
And I can view this mimic show of thee,
120   Time has but half succeeded in his theft,
Thyself removed, thy power to soothe me left.

Yardley Oak

Survivor sole, and hardly such, of all
That once lived here thy brethren, at my birth
(Since which I number threescore winters past)
A shattered veteran, hollow-trunked perhaps
5   As now, and with excoriate forks deform,
Relicts of ages! Could a mind imbued
With truth from heaven created thing adore,
I might with reverence kneel and worship thee.
It seems idolatry with some excuse
10   When our forefather druids in their oaks
Imagined sanctity. The conscience yet
Unpurified by an authentic act
Of amnesty, the meed of blood divine,
Loved not the light, but gloomy into gloom
15   Of thickest shades, like Adam after taste
Of fruit proscribed, as to a refuge, fled.

Thou was a bauble once; a cup and ball
Which babes might play with; and the thievish jay
Seeking her food, with ease might have purloined
20   The auburn nut that held thee, swallowing down
Thy yet close-folded latitude of boughs
And all thine embryo vastness, at a gulp.
But fate thy growth decreed. Autumnal rains
Beneath thy parent tree mellowed the soil
25   Designed thy cradle, and a skipping deer
With pointed hoof dibbling the glebe, prepared
The soft receptacle in which secure
Thy rudiments should sleep the winter through.
So Fancy dreams. Disprove it if ye can
30   Ye reasoners broad awake, whose busy searce
Of argument, employed too oft amiss,
Sifts half the pleasures of short life away.
Thou fell'st mature, and in the loamy clod
Swelling, with vegetative force instinct
35   Didst burst thine egg, as theirs the fabled twins
Now stars, two lobes protruding paired exact.
A leaf succeeded, and another leaf,
And all the elements thy puny growth
Fostering propitious, thou becam'st a twig.
40   Who lived when thou wast such? Oh could'st thou speak
As in Dodona once thy kindred trees
Oracular, I would not curious ask
The future, best unknown, but at thy mouth
Inquisitive, the less ambiguous past.
45   By thee I might correct, erroneous oft,
The clock of history, facts and events
Timing more punctual, unrecorded facts
Recovering, and mis-stated setting right.
Desperate attempt till trees shall speak again!
50   Time made thee what thou wast, king of the woods.
And Time hath made thee what thou art, a cave
For owls to roost in. Once thy spreading boughs
O'erhung the champain, and the numerous flock
That grazed it stood beneath that ample cope
55   Uncrowded, yet safe-sheltered from the storm.

No flock frequents thee now; thou has outlived
Thy popularity, and art become
(Unless verse rescue thee awhile) a thing
Forgotten as the foliage of thy youth.

60   While thus through all the stages thou hast pushed
Of tree-ship, first a seedling hid in grass,
Then twig, then sapling, and as century rolled
Slow after century, a giant bulk
Of girth enormous with moss-cushioned root
65   Upheaved above the soil, and sides embossed
With prominent wens globose, till at the last
The rottenness which Time is charged to inflict
On other mighty ones found also thee –
What exhibitions various hath the world
70   Witnessed of mutability in all
That we account most durable below!
      Change is the diet on which all subsist
Created changeable, and change at last
Destroys them. Skies uncertain, now the heat
75   Transmitting cloudless, and the solar beam
Now quenching in a boundless sea of clouds,
Calm and alternate storm, moisture and drought,
Invigorate by turns the springs of life
In all that live, plant, animal, and man,
80   And in conclusion mar them. Nature's threads,
Fine, passing thought, even in her coarsest works,
Delight in agitation, yet sustain
The force that agitates not unimpaired,
But worn by frequent impulse, to the cause
85   Of their best tone their dissolution owe.
      Thought cannot spend itself comparing still
The great and little of thy lot, thy growth
From almost nullity into a state
Of matchless grandeur, and declension thence
90   Slow into such magnificent decay.
Time was, when settling on thy leaf a fly
Could shake thee to the root, and time has been
When tempests could not. At thy firmest age
Thou hadst within thy bole solid contents

To the Nightingale which the Author Heard Sing on New Year's Day 1792

Whence is it that amazed I hear
    From yonder withered spray
This foremost morn of all the year
    The melody of May?

5 And why, since thousands would be proud
    Of such a favour shown,
Am I selected from the crowd
    To witness it alone?

Sing'st thou, sweet Philomel, to me
10   For that I also long
Have practised in the groves like thee,
    Though not like thee in song?

Or sing'st thou rather under force
    Of some divine command,
15 Commissioned to presage a course
    Of happier days at hand?

Thrice welcome then! for many a long
    And joyless year have I,
As thou today, put forth my song
20   Beneath a wintry sky.

But thee no wintry skies can harm,
    Who only need'st to sing
To make e'en January charm,
    And every season spring.

To Mary

The twentieth year is well-nigh past
Since first our sky was overcast,
Ah would that this might be the last
                My Mary!

5   Thy spirits have a fainter flow,
I see thee daily weaker grow –
'Twas my distress that brought thee low
                My Mary!

Thy needles once a shining store
10   For my sake restless heretofore
Now rust disused and shine no more
                My Mary!

For though thou gladly would'st fulfil
The same kind office for me still
15   Thy sight now seconds not thy will
                My Mary!

But well thou played'st the housewife's part
And all thy threads with magic art
Have wound themselves around this heart
20   My Mary!

Thy indistinct expressions seem
Like language uttered in a dream,
Yet me they charm whate'er the theme
                My Mary!

25   Thy silver locks once auburn bright
Are still more lovely in my sight
Than golden beams of orient light
                My Mary!

For could I view nor them nor thee,
30 What sight worth seeing could I see?
The sun would rise in vain for me
                    My Mary!

Partakers of the sad decline
Thy hands their little force resign,
35 Yet gently pressed press gently mine
                    My Mary!

And then I feel that still I hold
A richer store ten-thousand-fold
Than misers fancy in their gold
40   My Mary!

Such feebleness of limbs thou prov'st
That now, at every step, thou mov'st
Upheld by two, yet still thou lov'st
                    My Mary!

45 And still to love though pressed with ill,
In wintry age to feel no chill
With me is to be lovely still
                    My Mary!

But ah by constant heed I know
50 How oft the sadness that I show
Transforms thy smiles to looks of woe
                    My Mary!

And should my future lot be cast
With much resemblance of the past,
55 Thy worn-out heart will break at last
                    My Mary!

The Castaway

Obscurest night involved the sky,
　　The Atlantic billows roared,
When such a destined wretch as I
　　Washed headlong from on board
Of friends, of hope, of all bereft,
His floating home for ever left.

No braver chief could Albion boast
　　Than he with whom he went,
Nor ever ship left Albion's coast
　　With warmer wishes sent,
He loved them both, but both in vain,
Nor him beheld, nor her again.

Not long beneath the whelming brine
　　Expert to swim, he lay,
Nor soon he felt his strength decline
　　Or courage die away;
But waged with Death a lasting strife
Supported by despair of life.

He shouted, nor his friends had failed
　　To check the vessel's course,
But so the furious blast prevailed
　　That, pitiless perforce,
They left their outcast mate behind,
And scudded still before the wind.

Some succour yet they could afford,
　　And, such as storms allow,
The cask, the coop, the floated cord
　　Delayed not to bestow;
But he, they knew, nor ship nor shore,
Whate'er they gave, should visit more.

Nor, cruel as it seemed, could he
        Their haste, himself, condemn,
Aware that flight in such a sea
        Alone could rescue *them*;
35 Yet bitter felt it still to die
Deserted, and his friends so nigh.

He long survives who lives an hour
        In ocean, self-upheld,
And so long he with unspent power
40   His destiny repelled,
And ever, as the minutes flew,
Entreated help, or cried, Adieu!

At length, his transient respite past,
        His comrades, who before
45 Had heard his voice in every blast,
        Could catch the sound no more;
For then, by toil subdued, he drank
The stifling wave, and then he sank.

No poet wept him, but the page
50   Of narrative sincere
That tells his name, his worth, his age,
        Is wet with Anson's tear,
And tears by bards or heroes shed
Alike immortalise the dead.

55 I, therefore, purpose not or dream,
        Descanting on his fate,
To give the melancholy theme
        A more enduring date,
But misery still delights to trace
60 Its semblance in another's case.

No voice divine the storm allayed,
        No light propitious shone,
When, snatched from all effectual aid,

> We perished, each, alone;
> 65 But I, beneath a rougher sea,
> And whelmed in deeper gulfs than he.

NOTES ON THE POEMS

THOMAS GRAY

Ode on the Spring

Written June 1742 in response to an 'Ode on May' which Richard West (Gray's closest friend since their school days at Eton) had sent to Gray in early May. Published anonymously in the successful *Collection of Poems, by Several Hands* (3 vols., 1748), edited by the publisher and bookseller Robert Dodsley (ii, 265–7). Reprinted in 1753 *Designs*, and again in 1768 *Poems*, where Gray added the notes, and from which the text here is taken. The poem's range of allusion (further emphasized by Gray's 1768 notes) and use of 'poetic diction' aroused Samuel Johnson's disapproval – 'the language is too luxuriant, and the thoughts have nothing new' (*Life of Gray*, 1781). An evocation of classical landscape and literature (the 'Hours', line 1, conventionally attend on Venus, here invoked as inspirer of natural growth rather than as goddess of love; 'Attic', line 5, literally, from Attica in Greece) moves into a tissue of allusion to classical and English poets, in particular Virgil, Milton, Shakespeare and Pope. The highly-wrought tone is clearly deliberate, creating a world of self-conscious poetic isolation which Gray then undercuts in the closing stanza.

Ode on a Distant Prospect of Eton College

Probably written August 1742; published anonymously in a folio pamphlet for 6d. on 30 May 1747, the first of Gray's poems to appear in print. Reprinted in Dodsley's 1748 *Collection*, with the 'Ode on the Spring', ii, 261–4. The text here is that of 1768, when Gray added the notes and the Greek epigraph ('I am a man; a sufficient excuse for being unhappy'). Written soon after Richard West's death and the breakdown of Gray's friendship with Horace Walpole, the poem elaborates a poignant contrast between childhood and adulthood. The recent death of Gray's father (November 1741) and fall from power of Sir Robert Walpole, Horace's father, may also be relevant. The ode reworks the popular eighteenth-century genre of topographical poetry, replacing historical/social/political vision (which the shadow of Windsor Castle might lead one to expect) with a more subjective exploration of memory and experience. One of the earliest examples of 'Romantic' lyric, it is notable also for its rich and dramatic use of personification. Henry VI's reputation for sanctity (line 4) may derive from Shakespeare's *Richard III*, V. i. 4, and Pope's 'Windsor Forest', line 312, where he is described as 'the martyr-king'. 'Science' (line 3) means knowledge in general, and 'margent' (line 23) is archaic for 'margin'.

Sonnet [on the Death of Mr Richard West]

Written August 1742. It follows the 'Ode on a Distant Prospect of Eton College' in Gray's Commonplace Book, but was not published in Gray's lifetime; Mason first published it in the 1775 *Poems*, where he supplied the full title. The text here derives from the Commonplace Book. Richard West, close friend and correspondent of Gray's since Eton, had died 1 June 1742, aged twenty-five. Gray had sent West his 'Ode on the Spring' in early June, not knowing that West was then dead; Gray's letter containing the 'Ode' was returned to him unopened, and he learnt of West's death from an elegy he saw in a newspaper. Wordsworth attacked the artificial diction of many of the lines of the 'Sonnet' in his 1800 'Preface' to the *Lyrical Ballads*; subsequent criticism has concentrated on defending Gray against such charges. Roger Lonsdale (1969) observes in his edition of *The Complete Poems* that 'in part the diction is intended to evoke a Miltonic richness which contrasts with the barer language (approved by Wordsworth [lines 6–8, 13–14]) used to describe the poet's barren spiritual condition'. The poem's theme – nature's indifference to Gray's grief – recapitulates that of a poem, 'Ad Amicos', which West had sent to Gray on 4 July 1737 (actually an imitation of Tibullus, *Elegies*, III. v), anticipating just such indifference after his own death. 'Phoebus' (line 2), here the sun, evokes Apollo as the sun god, with resonances also of his status as god of youth and music or poetry; 'require' (line 6) carries the additional Latinate sense of 'to seek for'.

Ode to Adversity

Written August 1742; published in 1753 *Designs*. The text here is that of 1768 *Poems*, where its title became 'Hymn to Adversity', despite Gray's continued use of 'Ode' in his written instructions to Dodsley, the printer. In the 1768 *Poems*, it followed the 'Ode on a Distant Prospect of Eton College', to which it is probably intended as a response; the use of personification in both poems is striking. Samuel Johnson disparaged the former in his *Life of Gray*, preferring the 'poetical and rational' moral stoicism of the 'Ode to Adversity'. The epigram is from Aeschylus, *Agamemnon*, lines 176–7, and translates as 'Zeus, who leadeth mortals in the way of understanding, Zeus, who hath established as a fixed ordinance that wisdom comes by suffering'. Gray translates the Greek god into the Roman Jove. There is no particular classical source for the identification of Adversity as a 'daughter of Jove' (line 1). 'Gorgon' (line 35) functions as an adjective, invoking the monstrous appearance of the snake-haired Gorgons of Greek myth, of whom Medusa is the best known. It is more commonly applied to Athena, goddess of war. The 'vengeful band' (line 36) are probably the avenging Eumenides or Furies, prominent in the tragedies of Aeschylus; they contrast with the 'philosophic train' of personified virtues in lines 25–32.

Ode on the Death of a Favourite Cat

Written early 1747 in response to a letter from Horace Walpole, *c*. 22 February 1747, requesting an epitaph on one of his cats, recently deceased in this unfortunate manner. First printed in Dodsley's 1748 *Collection*, ii, 267–9. Revised for 1753 *Designs*, where it is winsomely illustrated. The text here is that of the 1768 *Poems*. The poem – disparaged by Johnson ('a trifle, but . . . not a happy trifle') – is essentially mock-heroic (invoking Milton's Eve, line 6, and Virgil's cupidinous Camilla from *Aeneid*, XI. 16–24, among others); also, as Roger Lonsdale (1969) observes, Gray introduces elements of animal fable, originating with Aesop and popular in the eighteenth century (e.g., Edward Moore's *Fables for the Female Sex*, 1744), which enable humorous moralizing beyond the scope of pure mock-heroic. Suvir Kaul (*Thomas Gray and Literary Authority*) has suggested that the poem is an anti-feminist satire on woman's appetite for luxury, but this seems questionable. 'Tyrian' (line 16) refers to the purple dye which derives from Tyre in the Mediterranean, and evokes antique splendour; a 'Nereid' (line 34) is a sea-nymph, and the Greek poet Arion was rescued by dolphins (line 34). 'Eight times' in line 31 alludes to the cat's proverbial nine lives.

Elegy Written in a Country Churchyard

Probably written between summer/autumn 1746, and June 1750. On 12 June 1750, Gray sent the poem to Horace Walpole; it circulated widely in manuscript form over the next few months. Hearing that the *Magazine of Magazines* planned to publish it, Gray and Walpole pre-emptively arranged with Dodsley for the 'Elegy' to be published on 15 February 1751. It was an instant success, with a 5th edition published before the end of 1751. Gray revised it for 1753 *Designs*; the text here is that of the 1768 *Poems*, when Gray added the three footnotes. They translate as follows: note 1, line 1, 'from afar he hears the chimes which seem to mourn for the dying day'; note 2, line 92, 'For I see in my thoughts, my sweet fire, one cold tongue and two beautiful closed eyes will remain full of sparks after our death'; and note 3, line 127, 'fearful hope'.

The composition history of the poem is complex. The earliest surviving manuscript, the 'Eton College MS', is more Christian/Stoic in tone than the final version; four stanzas which, according to Gray's friend and early editor, William Mason, concluded the much shorter first version of the poem, were excised by Gray from later expanded versions; their conventional pious consolation no doubt became inappropriate to the poem's growing complexity. These lines, following line 72 of the final version, were as follows:

> The thoughtless World to Majesty may bow
> Exalt the brave, & idolize Success
> But more to Innocence their Safety owe
> Than Power & Genius e'er conspired to bless
>
> And thou, who mindful of the unhonour'd Dead
> Dost in these Notes thy artless Tale relate
> By Night and lonely Contemplation led
> To linger in the gloomy Walks of Fate
>
> Hark how the sacred Calm, that broods around
> Bids ev'ry fierce tumultuous Passion cease
> In still small Accents whisp'ring from the Ground
> A grateful Earnest of eternal Peace
>
> No more with Reason & thyself at strife
> Give anxious Cares & endless Wishes room
> But thro' the cool sequester'd Vale of Life
> Pursue the silent Tenour of thy Doom.

As well as the removal of these stanzas, there are many other differences between the Eton College MS and the final version of the 'Elegy'; the interested reader should consult F. G. Stokes' edition of the *Elegy* (Oxford, 1929), which describes the manuscripts and early editions. See also the facsimile of the first edition and the Eton College MS, ed. George Sherburn, Augustan Reprint Society (Los Angeles, 1951); see also Lonsdale (1977).

Sources and influences are numerous, as Lonsdale (1969) makes clear. Here is a brief outline of these. The poem echoes classical celebrations of rural retirement, especially Virgil's *Georgics*, II. 458 ff, and Horace's second *Epode*; there is also the more recent influence of the so-called 'graveyard' poetry of the early–mid eighteenth century, such as Young's *Night Thoughts* (1742–6), Blair's *The Grave* (1743), and James Hervey's *Meditations among the Tombs* (1746); although Gray is much less melodramatic than these sources, the 'Elegy' does echo their Christian moralizing, which sits uneasily with the epistemology of the classical sources. William Collins' *Odes* (1746), and the nostalgic, romantic poetry of Thomas and Joseph Warton (*Five Pastoral Eclogues*, 1745, *The Pleasures of Melancholy*, 1747) and Mark Akenside (*The Pleasures of Imagination*, 1744) are also influences. As so often in Gray, Milton's presence is tangible, especially the elegiac Milton of 'Lycidas' (1638), and the moody figure of 'Il Penseroso' (1631) who, with Shakespeare and Spenser, help to build the image of Gray's solitary youth. Lines 33–6 were probably inspired by four lines in a 'Monody on the Death of Queen Caroline' by Richard West, printed in Dodsley's *Collection* (1748), ii. 269 ff.

Perhaps the best-remembered poem of the eighteenth century, the 'Elegy' was praised by Johnson for its universal appeal, its 'sentiments to which every bosom returns an echo'. This universal appeal has not, however, precluded critical controversy, much of which is usefully documented in Herbert W. Starr, *Twentieth-Century Interpretations of Gray's Elegy* (Englewood Cliffs, New Jersey, 1968). Debate has centred on the poem's tone and focus: is it shaped more by its classical or Christian poetic influences? Is it predominantly moral or socio-political? Is its primary concern the human condition, or the contrast between privilege and penury, or – more self-indulgently – the role and fate of the poet? Does it display love of the peasantry and estrangement from the gentry, or vice versa? Another major bone of contention is the identity of the 'youth' commemorated in the closing 'Epitaph', and apparently conflated with the narrator in lines 93–6 (the shift to 'thee' from the 'me' of stanza one is important here). Is he Gray himself, or a fictional narrator-poet? The concluding 'Epitaph' perhaps signifies a growing objective self-awareness on the part of the narrator-poet and, more expansively, uncertainty over the function of poetry at this point in history.

There are few – remarkably few – obscurities. The adjective 'storied' in line 41 suggests an urn wrought with figures so as to relate a history (Keats's 'Ode on a Grecian Urn' is a helpful comparison). Cleanth Brooks in 'Gray's Storied Urn' (1947; see Starr, 23–32) observes that there are 'actually more references to the details of the abbey church as a burial place than to the details of the country churchyard itself', and that the series of personifications, in lines 37–52 in particular, evoke the allegorical figures characteristic of eighteenth-century mortuary sculpture. John Hampden (1594–1643) (lines 57–8), a republican hero of the English Civil War, is linked here with Milton and Cromwell, lynch-pins of the anti-Royalist cause, whose greatness is indisputable but also perhaps destructive. Their names were substituted for the Roman originals (Cato, Tully, and Caesar) in the Eton College MS. 'Science' at line 119, as in the 'Ode on a Distant Prospect of Eton College', signifies knowledge or learning in general, and is here personified as one of the Muses.

A Long Story

Written between August and October 1750; the trial for highway robbery of Macleane (line 120), who had robbed among others Horace Walpole, in Hyde Park, took place on 13 September 1750. Printed in 1753 *Designs* – for the sake only of Bentley's illustrations, Gray claimed, and he carefully excluded it from the 1768 *Poems*. Johnson (*Life of Gray*, 1781) pronounced it 'an odd composition . . . which adds little to Gray's character'. The poem, in the manner of Matthew Prior (1664–1721), humorously inflates an encounter at Stoke Poges in August 1750. Anne, Lady Cobham, widow of Sir Richard Temple, 1st Viscount Cobham (d. 1749), with her niece Henrietta Speed and two friends, Lady Schaub (a Frenchwoman, hence the reference at line 25) and Lady Brown, a friend of Gray's, decided to pay Gray a visit, having read and admired the 'Elegy' in manuscript. The poet was out (or perhaps, as lines 69–72 suggest, in the garden shed or summer-house) and the women left a note (line 80) which, according to eighteenth-century etiquette, obliged him to return the visit. The Cobham residence, the Manor House at Stoke Poges, and its historic past, figure largely in the poem. Rebuilt in 1555 by Henry Hastings, Earl of Huntingdon (1535–95), it was probably then taken over by the Lord Chancellor, Sir Christopher Hatton (1540–91). Its Gothic architecture is evoked in lines 5–8, its lively former inhabitants are recalled in lines 9–16; and their ghosts appear as onlookers in lines 98–112 and 129–40, shocked at the modern familiarity between Lady Cobham and Gray. Robert Purt (line 41), clergyman and Fellow of King's College, Cambridge (d. 1752), had told Lady Cobham that the celebrated author of the 'Elegy' was staying nearby. In line 86, 'pothooks' punningly evoke instruments of punishment and the curved or hooked strokes made in handwriting; 'Phoebus', or Apollo (line 91) seems to be invoked for his martial rather than musical abilities. 'Here 500 stanzas are lost' (Gray's note) parodies – in a manner reminiscent of Swift and Pope – the device of the mutilated manuscript, and helpfully condenses the poem's action.

Stanzas to Mr Bentley

Written between 1751 and 1753, while Gray and Bentley were collaborating on the 1753 *Designs*. The text used here was first printed in 1775, in Mason's *Memoirs* of Gray. The words in square brackets are supplied by Mason, Gray's original manuscript (now lost) having a torn corner. Richard Bentley (1708–81), son of the famous Cambridge classical scholar loathed by Swift and Pope, was also collaborating with Horace Walpole on the 'Gothicizing' of his house at Strawberry Hill in the early 1750s. The poem begins as a fairly conventional exploration of the 'sister arts', poetry and painting (cf. Dryden's 'Epistle to Kneller' and Pope's 'Epistle to Jervas'), but modulates into a pessimistic vision of poetry's decline in Gray's time.

The Progress of Poesy. A Pindaric Ode

Written early 1750s. In 1752, Gray facetiously wrote to Walpole about his intention to produce 'a high Pindarick upon stilts' (*Corr.* i. 364). First published as 'Ode', with *The Bard*, in a quarto pamphlet on 8 August 1757 by Dodsley, the first book to be printed on Walpole's own press at Strawberry Hill. Reprinted in the 1768 *Poems* as 'The Progress of Poesy. A Pindaric Ode', with the text as used here. The 1757 version was unannotated, and, according to the epigraph from Pindar (*Olympian Odes*, II. 85), 'vocal to the Intelligent alone'. But in response to widespread puzzlement, Gray in his 1768 *Poems* supplied the notes which are here presented (unmodernized). He did not supply translations from the Greek, Latin or Italian. His notes translate as follows: line 35, 'with feet that seemed to twinkle as they moved'; line 41, 'and on his roseate cheeks there gleams the light of love'; line 54, 'beyond the paths of the year and the sun' (Virgil) and 'all remote from the solar road' (Petrarch); line 98, 'the flaming walls of the heavens'; line 102, '[the Muse] took away his sight, but she gave him sweet song'; line 115, 'against the godlike bird of Zeus'.

The 'Pindaric Ode' was first introduced into English poetry in Abraham Cowley's *Pindarique Odes* (1656), a misguided interpretation of the Greek poet Pindar (522–442 BC) as simply a passionate disregarder of metrical rules. Gray's versions – he was an accomplished classical scholar – are more faithful to Pindar's original structure and principles, involving a tripartite division, an allusive, wide-ranging narrative mode, and an interweaving of the public concerns of epic with the more private focus of the lyric. 'The Progress of Poesy' and 'The Bard' provoked intense reactions on publication. Whether admired – as by Walpole and Boswell ('I admire Gray prodigiously. I have read his odes till I was almost mad') – or despised for their 'cumbrous splendour' and 'strutting dignity', as by Johnson, they were found to be 'terribly obscure' (Goldsmith, in conversation with Boswell). Robert Lloyd and George Colman published successful parodies in 1760, 'An Ode to Obscurity' and 'An Ode to Oblivion'.

The poem opens with a celebration of the power of poetry to uplift (I. 1–3) or console (II. 1), and its global extent and dependence on political liberty (II. 2). Gray's note at line 54 alludes to the Gaelic or 'Erse' poetry of the ancient Scots 'discovered' (in fact forged) by James Macpherson in 1760; also to the more genuine ancient Welsh poetry unearthed in 1764 by

Evan Evans, an antiquarian scholar, and various fragments from Norse poetry, which Gray himself translated (see 'The Fatal Sisters', below). The poem then adopts a historical perspective (cf. James Thomson's *Liberty*, 1735–6 and William Collins' 'Ode to Liberty', 1746), relating the progress of the poetic muses, in the wake of political liberty, from Greece to Rome and thence to England, where they inspired Shakespeare, poet of the passions (personified in lines 92–5), the sublime Milton (lines 95–102), and the elegant vigour of Dryden (lines 103–6). The final stanza refers obliquely to Gray's own poetic ambitions, with a mixture of diffidence (lines 112–13) and moral assurance (line 123). The 'Good' and 'Great' distinction at line 123 evokes a growing distance between the virtuous poet and the public life of the nation.

In addition to those obscurities which Gray's notes illuminate, various references need glossing. The 'Aeolian lyre' at line 1 refers generally to an inspired mode of Greek music, rather than to the Aeolian wind-harp itself; 'Helicon' (line 3) was a mountain in Boeotia sacred to the Muses; 'Ceres' (line 9) is the goddess of harvest; 'Thracia's hills' (line 17) evoke Thracia, a region of Greece associated with Mars; 'Idalia' (line 27) was a town in Crete where Aphrodite, goddess of love also known as Cytherea after her island home (line 29), was worshipped. 'Hyperion' (line 53) was the Sun, or his father; 'Delphi' (line 66) was the ancient shrine of Apollo, the god of poetry, on Mount Parnassus (line 78). 'Ilissus' and 'Maeander' (lines 68–9) were both rivers in ancient Greece, and the 'sad Nine' (line 77) are the nine Muses. 'Latian' (line 78), from 'Latium', the region surrounding Rome, means 'Roman'; the reference to the 'Theban eagle' (line 115) evokes Pindar himself, who came from Thebes.

The Bard. A Pindaric Ode

Written between 1755 and May 1757; published 8 August 1757 with 'The Progress of Poesy'. Gray refused to annotate 'The Bard', like 'The Progress of Poesy', until the 1768 *Poems*, which published the text used here. Gray's 1768 notes are also given here. For the 'Pindaric' aspect of the poem, and its perceived obscurity, see note on p. 167 to 'The Progress of Poesy'. Its exploration of British bardic legend makes it an effective sequel to 'The Progress of Poesy'. The poem opens with the Bard denouncing Edward I as he returns, with his army and followers, from his suppression of Wales (Cambria) in 1283; Gray took the story from Thomas Carte's *General History of England* (1750). In lines 23–48, the speaker laments in particular the murder of his companion bards (whose names, beyond their Welshness, are not of great significance; 'Plinlimmon' at line 34 is a mountain). The bards' ghosts, invoked at line 44, chorus an extended visionary curse on the descendants of Edward I (lines 49–100). The curse is figured as an elaborate tapestry or 'tissue', as in 'The Fatal Sisters' (see below), which is, however, Nordic rather than Welsh. After their curse, the murdered bards vanish, and the Bard alone foresees the restoration of virtuous rule and political liberty with the accession of the Tudors. Under Queen Elizabeth (lines 115–24), British poetry revives, beginning with Shakespeare's 'buskined measures' ('buskined' means tragic, deriving from the 'buskin' or footwear worn by tragic actors). The Bard's defiant suicide at the culmination of his vision somewhat undercuts the poem's celebration of poetic power.

The Fatal Sisters. An Ode

Probably written 1761. Published in the 1768 *Poems*, with companion pieces 'The Descent of Odin. An Ode' (also from the Norse) and 'The Triumphs of Owen. A Fragment' (from the ancient Welsh), to replace 'A Long Story'. Gray translated 'The Fatal Sisters' from existing seventeenth-century Latin translations by Thorfaeus and Bartholin of the original (eleventh-century and onwards) Norse saga, *Njáls Saga*. Like Gray's translations from the Welsh, e.g. 'The Death of Hoël' (see below), 'The Fatal Sisters' originates, as the 'Advertisement' describes, in Gray's intermittent researches towards a 'History of English Poetry'. There are also obvious debts to Shakespeare's witches in *Macbeth*. Obscurities in the poem are not all of Gray's making; 'Randver' and his killers (line 8) are obscure in the Latin; the names of the Valkyries (lines 17–18, 31) derive from various translations of the original Norse. Orkney at line 8 simply refers to Sigurd, Earl of the Orkney Islands. Eirin (line 45) is Ireland.

[*The Death of Hoël*]

Written 1760 or 1761 but not included in the 1768 *Poems*. First printed by Mason (who supplies the title) in the 1775 *Poems*, from Gray's Commonplace Book, from where the text here derives. It is a translation from the Welsh poem 'Gododdin', fragments of which, surviving from the sixth century, Gray had seen in Latin translation by Evan Evans, the Welsh antiquarian scholar. As with 'The Fatal Sisters', the poem derives from Gray's interest in early sources of English poetry. The Gododdin of the poem's title were an ancient North British tribe whose leader sent 300 warriors to recapture Catterick in North Yorkshire ('Cattraeth') from the forces of Deira, a Saxon kingdom in North East Yorkshire. *The Death of Hoël* is a lament by the Gododdin's bard Aneurin, sole survivor of the doomed attack. The names at lines 6–7 and 21, obviously denoting Gododdin warriors, are obscure.

[Sketch of His Own Character]

Written 1761; first printed, from Gray's manuscript, by Mason (who supplied the title), in his *Memoirs* of Gray (1775). Line 5 seems to allude to Gray's refusal of the Poet Laureateship in 1757; its proud independence seems deliberately to recall that of the later Pope (see 'Imitations of Horace', Satire II. i. 116 and Epistle II. i. 371). Charles Townshend (1725–67) had been appointed Secretary at War on 24 March 1761. He was not noted for his integrity; similarly, Dr Samuel Squire (1713–66) was an ambitious and disreputable cleric who was appointed Bishop of St David's on 14 April 1761.

The Candidate

Probably written between January and March 1764. The poem is a much sharper satire than Churchill's of the same title and target, but Gray's was not published until several years after the events satirized. Gray had read and also annotated earlier attacks by Churchill, including 'The Conference', on the Earl of Sandwich, the target of 'The Candidate' poems (see Edmund Gosse, 'Gray's notes on Churchill', *Transactions of the Royal Society of Literature*, xxxvi (1918), 161–79). Gray's 'Candidate' was first printed in the *London Evening Post*, February 1777; the text here is from a separately published flysheet, of uncertain date, with the final word supplied from a copy in Walpole's hand (now in the Pierpont Morgan Library), which the flysheet otherwise follows closely.

John Montagu (1718–92), 4th Earl of Sandwich, 1st Lord of the Admiralty, a principal Secretary of State, and a notorious debauchee, put himself forward for the High Stewardship of the University of Cambridge late in 1763. Sandwich had recently denounced his former friend John Wilkes in the House of Lords (15 November 1763) for his obscene poem, the *Essay on Woman*, thus adding hypocrisy to his sins. Sandwich's candidacy for the Stewardship was backed by the crown, and this complicated the University's instinctive revulsion from him. His nickname of 'Jemmy Twitcher' (line 1) was current at the time, deriving from Gay's *Beggar's Opera* (1728); 'twitcher' was slang for 'pick-pocket'. The world of Gay's opera is again invoked at line 17, Newgate being London's jail, and a 'Newgate-bird' a persistent offender. Jemmy Twitcher's wooing of the 'Three Sisters', Physic (Medicine), Law and Divinity, refers to Sandwich's cultivation of the three Cambridge faculties; the latter, populated by clergymen anxious for preferment, offered him the most support, prompting Gray to the portrait of lewd self-serving in lines 23–34. The reference at line 8 to Sandwich's nose hints at the effects of syphilis; at line 12 Gray draws a pointed comparison with the notorious libertine poet, John Wilmot (1647–80), 2nd

Earl of Rochester; line 14 alludes to the alleged lunacy and confinement of Sandwich's wife. The 'band' at line 22 seems to refer to clerical garb. Lines 23–30 are a parodic exercise in justification through biblical precedent, invoking David, author of the Psalms; the sexual vigour of King Solomon; the activities of the Israelites in *Exodus*, 12:35–6; the prophet of Bethel who lied (with obscure motivation) with impunity in *1 Kings* 13:11–19; and Noah's drunkenness (*Genesis*, 4:21). The poem's final word – supplied only by Walpole – unsettled Gray's early editors; Walpole and Mason both proposed alternative closing couplets. 'Stitch' carries almost the weight of the 'f-word' in modern parlance.

On L[or]d H[olland']s Seat near M[argat]e, K[en]t

Written June 1768; published, without Gray's permission, in *The New Foundling Hospital for Wit*, iii, 34–5 (1769), perhaps derived from a copy in the hand of Gray's friend, Thomas Warton (now in the British Museum), the source for the text here.

Henry Fox (1705–74), Lord Holland, had once been admired by Gray for his aggressive foreign policy, but had then bribed or intimidated other MPs to support the 1763 Peace of Paris. In 1767, Holland himself printed a poem, *Lord Holland returning from Italy 1767*, berating his former colleagues for deserting him: Gray's poem parodies Holland's, making much also of the grotesque landscape and deliberately ruined architecture of Holland's estate at Kingsgate, near Margate. The Goodwin Sands (line 6), marking the entrance to the Straits of Dover, are named after the Saxon Earl Godwin. John Stuart (1713–92), 3rd Earl of Bute (line 17), was Chief Minister to George III, 1760–63 and widely hated; William Petty (1737–1805), 2nd Earl of Shelburne (line 18), was President of the Board of Trade in 1763; Richard Rigby (1722–88) held several Treasury positions; John Calcraft (1726–72) was allegedly Holland's bastard son, and also influential in treasury politics: all these men eventually quarrelled with Holland, whose penchant for ravaged landscape becomes a metaphor for his destructive ambition. As Suvir Kaul (*Thomas Gray and Literary Authority*) has observed, Gray here speaks in Pope's satirical idiom, representing individuals as agents of wider cultural destruction.

CHARLES CHURCHILL

The Apology. Addressed to the Critical Reviewers

Written between March and May 1761. Published May 1761 in a one-shilling quarto pamphlet. Four further editions published in 1761, and a 6th in 1763. The text is that of the first edition.

The motto derives punningly from Horace, *Odes*, Book I, Ode 26, which has 'Creticum' instead of 'Criticum' and translates as 'Dear to the Muses, I will banish gloom and fear to the wild winds to carry over the Cretan sea'. The pun had first been made by Steele in *Tatler*, 10 (1709).

The poem is prompted by the *Critical Review*'s inept and hostile review of Churchill's 'The Rosciad' (March 1761), which satirized the London theatre, and the playwright Arthur Murphy (1727–1805) in particular. The *CR* had attributed 'The Rosciad' to Churchill's friends, Robert Lloyd, George Colman and Bonnell Thornton. Although the *CR* later apologized for this error, Churchill riposted with 'The Apology', whose main targets were Murphy again (whom Churchill suspected of writing the original review), and Tobias Smollett (1721–71), novelist and then editor of the *Critical Review* (and later a prominent supporter of Bute).

'The Apology' falls into three movements. The first (lines 1–169) attacks the tyranny of the reviews, especially the *CR*, whose printer, Archibald Hamilton, is mentioned at line 43. The allusion in line 86 to 'Dullness', the goddess of Pope's mock-epic *The Dunciad* (1728–43), signals Churchill's debt to Pope's satire on the book trade. In lines 132–9 Churchill satirizes the *CR*'s mistaken attribution of 'The Rosciad' ('The Actor', mentioned at line 135, was a poem by Lloyd, published April 1760, which partly inspired 'The Rosciad'; Colman's play, *The Jealous Wife* [line 137] was a success in 1761). Lines 308–11 return to the theme of this first movement, parodying the *CR*'s disapproval of 'The Rosciad''s attack. Smollett himself is a frequent target; at line 68 he is likened to Drawcansir, a character in Buckingham's play *The Rehearsal* (1672), who slays 'both friend and foe'. A translation of Voltaire to which Smollett put his name (although most of it was made by Thomas Francklin) is attacked in lines 70–82, where Smollett is represented as a murderously inaccurate translator. Voltaire had been exiled from France for his radical opinions and was then resident in Switzerland (lines 71–8). The anonymity of book reviews in the *CR*, which, like the *Monthly Review*, appeared monthly (lines 191–2) is attacked at line 110. Smollett is the probable target of the attack on the monstrous critic in lines 298–313. He is certainly the subject of the satire at lines 150–55; these refer to Fielding's *Covent Garden Journal*, 2 (7 January 1752), which presents a mock heroic battle between 'General Thomas Jones' (alluding to Fielding's *Tom Jones* of 1749) and 'Peeragrin Puckle' (alluding to Smollett's *Peregrine Pickle*, 1751), in which the latter is defeated. The success of Fielding's farce *Tom Thumb* (1730) (line 155) is contrasted with the dismal failure of Smollett's heroic tragedy *The Regicide* (satirized in lines 156–69), which was never performed but was published in 1749. Smollett's activities as a historian, especially of the *Complete History of England*, published in many volumes, 1757–65, are ridiculed in lines 152–3, where he is ironically compared to the great historian of Rome, Livy.

The second movement of the poem (lines 170–297), prefaced by the attack on *The Regicide*, satirizes popular drama and entertainments of the day, draws parallels between jumped-up strolling players and critics, and makes personal attacks on Murphy. Murphy's attack on Churchill, 'An Ode to the Naiads of Fleet Ditch' (1761) is ridiculed from line 170, as is his tendency to import Gallicisms (in, for example, his tragedy *The Orphan of China*; allegations that he plagiarized this from Voltaire are alluded to in lines 231–5). The hybrid quality of Murphy's writing is suggested in lines 174–5; 'linsey-woolsey' is a cloth made of wool and flax, here implying a mish-mash; Joseph's coat was similarly various (*Genesis* 33:3). Murphy is attacked again at lines 178–85, where his poetic drama, *The Desert Island*, whose heroine Sylvia indulges in sickly hyperbole, is parodied. More generally, lines 186–225 and 234–83 satirize the extremes of contemporary theatre. Lines 200–205 evoke the three-day puppet and pantomime festival of St Bartholomew Fair in London's Smithfield, during which a character based on Smollett's Peregrine Pickle made a brief appearance. Strolling players, who risked arrest as vagabonds unless they could win over the local Mayor or Justice of the Peace (lines 206–11), are contrasted with the commercial theatre's fondness for display and bombast (lines 212–25). Line 225 evokes recent flamboyant productions of Nathaniel Lee's *The Rival Queens* (1677) and *Romeo and Juliet* (to which Garrick added a funeral procession scene in 1753). Lines 256–9 allude to public lectures on oratory given by the actor Charles Macklin (1699?–1797) and the actor manager Thomas Sheridan (1719–88), which Churchill had also satirized in 'The Rosciad'. Lines 266–75 attack the powerful actor, playwright and theatre manager, David Garrick (1717–79), whom Churchill had praised in 'The Rosciad' (gaining however little thanks for his pains) and whose tyrannical ambitions are now contrasted with Churchill's own commitment to independence (lines 270–75). The 'playhouse freedom' of line 269 refers to the theatre managers' dispensing of free tickets to friends, playwrights and critics.

The final section of the poem (lines 276–421) is mainly concerned with the true end of poetry, its alliance with truth and virtue, and Churchill's stylistic predecessors, Edmund Waller (1606–87), Alexander Pope (1688–1744), and, pre-eminently, John Dryden (1631–1700). Their vigour is contrasted to current insipid fashions, epitomized by the vogue for Italian castrati singers (lines 346–9). An imagined critique of Churchill's poetic activities, given his clerical vocation (lines 390–93), recommends that he emulate Thomas Sternhold (d. 1549) who, with John Hopkins (d. 1570), versified the Psalms, and became a byword for dullness.

There are some allusions to classical and biblical mythology and history: 'Astraea' at line 12 is the goddess of justice; 'Pompey' at line 80 is Gnaeus Pompeius (106–48 BC), defeated by Julius Caesar at Pharsalius, but finally murdered in Egypt; the 'Stagyrite' at line 91 is Aristotle, born in Stageira, 384 BC, to whose *Poetics* Churchill is referring; lines 104–5 refer to the Israelites' worship of the golden calf in *Exodus*, 32; Procrustes (line 361) was a villainous individual in ancient Greece who, having invited passing travellers to rest the night with him, would either stretch them or chop off their extremities so that they would fit into his bed.

Some eighteenth-century idioms and proper names need glossing; 'puffs off' (line 24) means 'praises extravagantly'; 'candour', used throughout, was a ubiquitous term, meaning 'kindness', 'favourable disposition' or 'leniency of judgement'; a 'Merry Andrew' at line 205 had come to mean a 'clown' or 'buffoon'; 'coffee-sages' and 'paper leading-strings' at lines 396–7 are obscure, but perhaps refer to the habit of newspaper-reading in coffee houses. Hannah Pritchard (line 290) was an actress (1711–68), and Charlotte Brent (line 375) a singer (d. 1802).

The Conference

Probably written October–November 1763. Published November 1763 in a quarto pamphlet for 2s. 6d. – a high price, as the *Critical Review*, 16 (1763), 443–6, observed, while pronouncing the poem 'a nervous, manly, and well-written performance'. The text is that of 1763, but 'me' in line 384 is an emendation from the original 'him', added in 1766 *Poems* (3rd edn.).

The poem's dialogue form, and discussion of human nature, clearly owes much to Pope, as does the poet's stance of proud independence; lines 129–52 thank that 'public' whose enthusiastic purchase of 'The Rosciad' had procured Churchill freedom from the need for patronage. 'Independence' in this context evinces a shift in meaning from land-based, 'Country' self-sufficiency, to a more democratic and general freedom.

The main debate within the poem is between Churchill and an unnamed 'Lord' who, once they have toasted the king (line 5) urges him to abandon principle and 'Virtue', and pursue his better interests by supporting whoever is in power – as do the poets James Ralph (1705?–62), who had abandoned his criticisms of the ministry in exchange for an annual pension of £300, and Paul Whitehead (1710–74), once a supporter of Wilkes but now in the pay of Bute. Although Churchill rejects this proposal with force, the Lord's bleak, Mandevillean view of human nature and self-interest ('Self is all in all', line 178) is powerfully presented.

Politically, the poem's immediate context is Wilkes's arraignment in the House of Lords for his obscene *Essay on Woman*, and the House of Commons having voted that the *North Briton* 45 was a 'seditious libel', on 15 November 1763. The *dramatis personae* are largely politicians; self-serving Court ministers and toadies on the one hand, and men of principle and pro-Wilkes sympathies on the other. 'Hirco' at lines 55–72 is John Stuart, 3rd Earl of Bute, First Lord of the Treasury (also mentioned at line 299); the reference to bed-staining alludes to the popular belief that Bute was the lover of the Princess Dowager. A frequent target of Churchill's satire, Bute was an unpopular Scot who devoted himself to increasing the power of the monarchy. He was the main target of the *North Briton*, which Wilkes and Churchill edited 1762–3. The sneer at Scotland (line 292) is part of Churchill's anti-Bute typography, as is the reference at lines 302–4 to Bute's creation of sixteen new, pro-Court, peers within two years in an attempt to strengthen the Crown's power in Parliament. William Murray, 1st Earl of Mansfield (1705–93) (line 40), another Scot, was Lord Chief Justice in Bute's ministry, notorious for his absolutist views on the authority of judges. Sir Fletcher Norton (1716–89) (lines 316 and 356) was appointed Attorney General in 1763; a virulent campaigner against Wilkes, he was largely responsible for *North Briton* 45 being voted a seditious libel in the House of Commons. At line 352, Churchill imagines Mansfield and Norton displaced by the still more draconian 'Judge Jeffreys' (George Jeffreys, 1st Baron Jeffreys of Wem, 1648–89), infamous for his harsh sentencing of the Monmouth rebels in 1688. Lines 254–61 offer a list of turncoat or hypocrite politicians; line 254 perhaps refers to William Pulteney, Earl of Bath (1684–1764), a prominent opponent of Sir Robert Walpole's ministry in the 1730s who had nevertheless accepted a peerage in 1742; lines 255–6 refer to John Montagu, 4th Earl of Sandwich (1718–92), a former libertine friend of Wilkes who had denounced the *Essay on Woman* in the House of Lords on 15 November 1763. He was satirized by both Churchill and Gray as 'The Candidate' for the office of High Steward of the University of Cambridge in 1764. William Warburton (1698–1779), Bishop of Gloucester (and Pope's literary executor) (line 258), a frequent butt of Churchill's satire, was a Tory who had seconded Sandwich's denunciation of Wilkes. Henry Fox (1705–74), Paymaster General to the Forces under Bute, an unscrupulous and treacherous politician, is attacked at line 299. In the 1765 *Poems*, his name becomes 'Holland'; he was created Baron Holland of Foxley, Wiltshire, on 16 April 1763. The virtuous politicians mentioned in the poem include Richard Grenville-Temple, Earl Temple (1711–79), Pitt's brother-in-law; a supporter of Wilkes, he lost his post as lord-lieutenant of Buckinghamshire as a result. William Petty, 1st Marquis of Lansdowne, Lord Shelburne (1737–1805), and John Calcraft (1726–72), although himself Fox's nephew, resisted Fox's demands for a peerage as a reward for leading the House of Commons in support of Bute's peace proposals in 1762. William Pitt, 1st Earl of Chatham (1708–78), whose resignation had made way for Bute, is himself mentioned at line 180; in lines 180–82, the Lord imputes selfish motives to Churchill's heroes (Pitt, and the line of William of Orange, 'Nassau', whose accession in 1688 was bound up with the guarantee of English political liberty) and villains (Bute, and the dispossessed line of Stuart kings, associated with Catholic and absolutist tendencies, mentioned again at lines 333 and 361–75), alike. The house of Brunswick (line 340) is that of the Georges I, II and III, to whom Churchill and his 'Patriot friends' (line 349) profess loyalty (lines 341–60), thus emphasizing that the quarrel is with corrupt ministers, not the monarch. The implicit 'Patriot' political hero of the poem is, of course, John Wilkes (line 300), MP for Aylesbury, anti-Bute campaigner, whose arrest for seditious libel provoked a huge controversy over the legality of 'general warrants' for arrest, and a wave of support for 'Wilkes and liberty' (closely allied to the 'independence' celebrated in this poem).

Autobiographical detail is woven into the poem; at lines 101–18, Churchill recalls being saved from debtors' prison by Pierson Lloyd (1704?–81), the father of his friend Robert Lloyd (1733–64). And at lines 213–26, he berates himself for his recent elopement (October 1763) with Elizabeth Carr, the fifteen-year-old daughter of a Westminster tradesman (the couple continued to live together after the scandal).

Biblical and literary allusion is used to heighten moments of crisis: in particular, lines 112–18 refer to *Matthew* 14 where Christ walks on the water, rescues Simon Peter, and allays the storm; line 231 refers to *Daniel* 5:5–26, and the writing on the wall in Belshazzar's palace, 'Thou art weighed in the balances, and art found wanting'; line 290 invokes the casting out of Cain, doomed to be 'a fugitive and a vagabond' in *Genesis* 4:12, and line 291 seems to echo Marlowe's *Doctor Faustus* (1588?), 'Hell hath no limits nor is circumscribed / In one self place, where we are is Hell, / And where Hell is, there must we ever be' (II. i. 120–2), and Milton's *Paradise Lost* (1667), 'The mind is its own place, and in it self / Can make a Heaven of Hell, a Hell of Heaven' (I. 254–5).

Some eighteenth-century idiom which may be obscure includes a 'dun' (lines 37 and 130), who was a debt collector; the use of 'Country' and 'Court' (line 159), which refers to basic divisions in the House of Commons between country gentlemen and supporters of the 'Court' (these divisions did not fully correlate with Whig/Tory ones); the 'Star' at line 305 refers to the symbol on the Order of the Garter, instituted by Edward III on St George's Day in 1350. For 'candour' (line 149), see note to 'The Apology'.

The Crab

Written between 1762 and 1764. Not published until Lance Bertelson presented it in ' "The Crab": An Unpublished Poem by Charles Churchill', *Philological Quarterly*, 30, (1984), 255–65. The text here derives from its only manuscript source, a letter to Wilkes in the Wilkes–Churchill correspondence in the British Museum.

The motto bowdlerizes Virgil, *Georgics* I. 34–5, and in its travestied form here translates as 'for thee the blazing crab contracts his claws'.

Bertelson suggests that the poem was written to amuse the libertine circle of Sir Francis Dashwood's 'Monks of Medmenham', of whom Churchill (briefly) and Wilkes were members. 'The Crab' presents a bawdy Chaucerian twist to the popular eighteenth-century genre of moral tale or fable, such as Gay's *Fables* (2 vols., 1727 and 1738) and (alluded to at line 131) Thomas D'Urfey's *Tales* (1704). The interweaving of sex and religion is characteristic of Churchill, who prefers his own libertine frankness about such matters to the hypocrisy indulged in by other clergymen; such as George Stone (line 2 and throughout), Archbishop of Armagh and Anglican Primate of Ireland, satirized as a homosexual by Churchill in 'The Times', lines 475–6, and in the 'Advertisement' to Wilkes's *Essay on Woman*. Stone was brother of Andrew Stone, an ally of Bute, and former tutor to George III.

There are some classical, literary and contemporary allusions, essentially facetious. The 'Pomonqué Queen' at line 72 is probably Pomona, Roman goddess of gardens and fruit trees, whose irrigating activities are here configured obscenely; the 'Florimel' of line 93 probably alludes to the incident in Spenser's *Faerie Queene* (1590–96), Book III. viii. 25–31, where the virgin Florimell is almost raped by a fisherman. Joshua Ward (1685–1761), mentioned in line 34, was a notorious quack and vendor of miracle pills.

The Times

Probably written during 1764. Published September 1764; like 'The Conference', in a quarto pamphlet for 2s. 6d. The text is that of the first edition. In a letter to Churchill dated 14 September 1764, Wilkes praises 'The Times', 'which I admire almost beyond any even of your pieces. You have greatly excell'd *Juvenal* in his own manner'. The *Critical Review*, 18 (1764), 198–203, was taken aback by the poem's subject matter: 'We are even somewhat doubtful whether it is fair for a satirist to attack crimes that are capital by law', referring to the status of homosexual activity at this time. William Cowper, in a letter to William Unwin in 1780, expresses admiration for the poem's energies, 'except that the Subject is disgusting to the last Degree'. 'The Times' is a sustained attack on the luxury and sexual excesses of Churchill's day, in particular the ubiquitous evil – as he saw it – of homosexuality. Lines 1–176 describe England's moral decline from an unspecified golden age of modesty and virtue; lines 1–2 seem to echo the opening of Dryden's *Absalom and Achitophel* (1681), which had celebrated Charles II's heterosexual vigour. Lines 177–254, with echoes of Pope's 'Dunciad' IV, rehearse the luxurious vices which England has imported from abroad. The association between foreign trade and travel, and luxury and decadence, was a commonplace of eighteenth-century thought, especially evident in Smollett, in particular *The Expedition of Humphry Clinker* (1771). Lines 21–2 refer to the threat posed to the English textile industry by the importation of luxury French textiles after the 1763 Peace of Paris; the peace was unpopular, and 'Economy' in line 30 refers ironically to the pacifist tendencies of Bute's and later Grenville's ministries. Similarly, lines 197–200 refer to the widely despised territorial concessions (particularly in the colonies) granted to France in 1763. The profligate 'Faber' (lines 55–102) is perhaps George Montagu Dunk, 2nd Earl of Halifax (1716–71), a prominent minister and one of Wilkes's persecutors; lines 71–6 allude, with hostility, to the peerage's immunity from arrest in civil matters, especially debt, and lines 95–102 glance ironically at the Court's claims to piety.

Italy (lines 219–54) and the East (lines 255–72) are especially blamed for the spread of homosexual activity in England, and the devaluing of women, whose attractions Churchill lists with enthusiasm (lines 273–334). Lines 235–40 are an attack on Italian castrati singers, one of Churchill's bugbears (cf. 'The Apology', lines 346–9). The pornographic etchings or 'postures' of Pietro Aretino (1492–1556) (line 242) enjoyed a clandestine popularity in England throughout the seventeenth and eighteenth centuries.

In the manner of Pope, Churchill then narrows his focus to a series of individual character sketches, interspersed with warnings to vulnerable young men on the threshold of homosexual whoredom (lines 431–524, 611–58). The poet then asserts his moral obligation to denounce such activity, and in the poem's closing lines again celebrates women as the source of national virtue.

Several of the names in the poem, whether real or assigned, are obscure, and probably refer to persons whose sexual incontinence was common knowledge in the 1760s, but has not been recorded in the more orthodox annals of history. A few blank spaces were filled in by Wilkes on a copy of Churchill's *Poems*, now in the British Library. Some names can be identified: John, 1st Earl Ligonier (1680–1770) (lines 148, 558, 578), was a field marshal in the British army who allegedly married a great fortune when in his dotage; for John Montagu, 4th Earl of Sandwich (1718–92) (lines 170 and, if Wilkes's identification is reliable, 562), see note to 'The Conference'; Lumley (line 288) may be the Hon. James Lumley, whipped by a Mrs Mackinsy in 1761, according to Horace Walpole; Aynam and Stroud (lines 339–40 and 494) are identified in Wilkes's notes, but remain otherwise obscure; Apicius (line 349 onward) obviously represents a nobleman of some fame, but no precise identity; perhaps he is Richard Child, 1st Earl Tylney of Castlemaine (1680–1750), or his son John, 2nd Earl (1712–84); Tylney is named again at lines 487–92. James Quin (1693–1766) (line 366) was a former actor and a famous gourmand; lines 403–5 refer to Thomas

Pelham-Holles, 1st Duke of Newcastle (1693–1768) and his renowned French cook, St Clouet. For Stone (line 476), see note to 'The Crab'. Hervey (line 485), identified in Wilkes's annotations, may be Thomas Hervey (1699–1775), an eccentric author whose marital affairs (including attempted divorce) were irregular; Barrowby (line 486) may be William Barrowby, physician (1682–1751), described by *DNB* as 'a monster of lewdness and prophaneness'. Sackville (line 494) is so identified by Wilkes, and may refer to George Sackville Germain, 1st Viscount Sackville (1716–85), military leader and subsequently an MP, but not especially renowned for sexual irregularity. Tyrawley (lines 559–61) is James O'Hara, Baron Kilmaine and 2nd Baron Tyrawley (1690–1773), field marshal and diplomat, at one point in Russia (hence the reference to Czarina Catherine the Great), who accumulated three wives and fourteen children. William Dodd (1729–77) (lines 575–7) was chaplain, of dubious morals, to London's Magdalen House charity for reformed prostitutes, near (though not in) Wellclose Square. The morally unexceptionable Mary Lepel (d. 1768) (line 607), to whom Pope addressed some occasional verses, married John, Baron Hervey of Ickworth (1696–1743) in 1720; their daughter was Caroline (line 610) (1736–1819). 'B—' at line 619, and 'H—' and 'M—' at line 638 remain obscure. Several of the assigned names are merely conventional, and have no apparent significance; Clodius (line 386), Corydon (line 430), Florio (line 481).

Allusions to the classical and biblical worlds include the following: Cain (lines 133–4) slew Abel his brother, 'and the Lord set a mark upon Cain, lest any finding him should kill him', thus dooming him to wander the earth (*Genesis* 4:15); 'Legion' (line 224) alludes to the man possessed by many spirits in *Mark* 5:9; Sappho (line 246) was a poetess on the Greek island of Lesbos, *c.* 600 BC, from where the term 'lesbian' derives; Ganymede (line 332) was a beautiful youth abducted and loved by Zeus; Hylas (line 333) suffered a similar fate at the hands of Heracles. Janus (line 428) was the two-faced Roman deity, who kept watch both ways over doors; the reference to 'Saint Socrates' at line 480 seems to be a jibe at the ancient Greeks' sexual proclivities; Diana (line 488) is goddess of chastity; the 'light-footed Greek' at line 513 is Achilles, schooled by the centaur Chiron; Achilles wept for his slain friend Patroclus in Homer's *Iliad*, XVIII. Narcissus (line 586) was a beautiful youth desired by both sexes, who fell in love with his own reflection (Ovid, *Metamorphoses*, III. 339–510). 'Augusta' at line 508 is an ancient name for London; see Dryden's 'Mac Flecknoe', lines 64–5.

Eighteenth-century idioms which may now be obscure include the following: 'guttling' (line 14), which Johnson's *Dictionary* glossed as 'feeding luxuriously, gormandising'; to 'cog the die' (line 28) means to fraudulently control the fall of a die or dice; 'runs out in' (line 66) means 'expends lavishly'; the phrase 'like Persians to the sun' (line 83) alludes to the popular belief that eastern religions were sun-worshipping; 'camps' (line 115) can refer either to military encampments or, more generally, to the makeshift dwellings of the poor; 'trucks' (line 137) means 'barters'; a 'bawd' (lines 150, 574) is a prostitute's 'madam', in modern parlance; 'mart' (line 162) is a marketplace; 'cates' (line 395) are dainty foodstuffs; 'varlet' (line 399) is a menial servant, not necessarily a term of abuse; 'jennet' (line 548) may mean a light horse, or a civet cat, but is obscure in this context; 'pathicks' (line 555) are males who submit to sodomy; presumably they relish the 1753 Marriage Act because it made marriage more difficult. The 'dog star' (line 567)is Sirius, in the constellation of the Greater Dog, brightest of the stars, thought to cause madness in conjunction with the heat of high summer. The Bridewell (line 573) was London's house of correction. The 'sables' at line 613 are black drapes which signify mourning. The 'king's evil' (line 625) is scrofula, believed to be curable by the monarch's touch (though this practice had died out after the reign of Queen Anne, d. 1714).

The Journey: A Fragment

Apparently unfinished at the time of Churchill's death; published April 1765 by Churchill's brother John, in a separate one-shilling quarto as well as in volume two of *Poems*, 1765. The text is that of the 1765 pamphlet.

Lines 1–30 seem to owe something to Swift's 'Verses on the Death of Dr Swift' (1739); lines 30–86 are more reminiscent of the later Pope in their exploration, through dialogue, of the poetic itch. 'Flexney' at line 82 is Churchill's own publisher, William Flexney (1731?–1808). Lines 99 to the end conjure a host of eighteenth-century authors from whom Churchill chooses to distance himself; in particular, over-learned writers, and Scots; the 'Tweed' (line 136) is the river separating England and Scotland, and 'fond of power' in line 119 is a jibe at the infiltration of Scots (Bute, Mansfield, and their lackeys) into positions of power under George III. 'Economist' (line 60) refers ironically to the pacifist policies of Bute, see note to 'The Times', line 30. William Mason (1724–97) (line 100) was the friend and literary executor of Gray (line 99): Gray's and Mason's odes had been parodied by Colman and Lloyd in 1760 ('An Ode to Obscurity' and 'An Ode to Oblivion'); Churchill had also mocked Mason's dramatic poems in 'The Rosciad' (lines 179–90). Mason's *Elegies* (1763) were criticized for their affected style by *Monthly Review*, 27 (1763), 486. Thomas Francklin (1721–84) (line 101) was a bumptious Professor of Greek at Cambridge, 1750–59: he published a translation of Sophocles in 1759 and was mocked by Lloyd in *Shakespeare: An Epistle to Mr Garrick* (1760). Richard Glover (line 103) was the author of tragedies on the Greek model, including *Leonidas* (1737) and *Medea* (1761), which were never intended for performance. Robert Dodsley (1703–64) wrote *Cleone*, a tragedy performed in 1758 which caused the audience, and Dodsley himself, to weep profusely (lines 103–6). William Whitehead (1715–85) (line 107) was Poet Laureate from 1757; he wrote several successful plays, including *The School of Lovers* (1762), which he himself acknowledged was adapted from Fontenelle's *Le Testament*. John Brown (1715–66) (line 109) published *An Estimate of the Manners and Principles of the Times* (1757) and an Ode, 'The Cure of Saul' (1763). For Arthur Murphy (line 111), see note to 'The Apology'. Samuel Foote (1720–77) (line 113) was a dramatist, actor and self-publicist; Churchill had satirized him in 'The Rosciad', and Foote in retaliation had caricatured Churchill in a revised version of his play, *Taste* (1761). 'Ossian' at line 121 is James Macpherson (1736–96), who presented as a 'translation' from the Gaelic an epic poem by 'Ossian', a Gaelic bard, entitled 'Fingal' (1762), and another, 'Temora' (1763), both patronized by Bute; they were an overnight success, admired by Gray but scorned by Johnson, and controversy over their authenticity did nothing to diminish their popularity. David Hume (1711–76) (line 122), philosopher and historian, published a *History of Great Britain under the Stuarts* (2 vols., 1754–7), and a *History of England under the House of Tudor* (4 vols., 1759–63), which aroused Churchill's ire because of their Tory vision. John Home (1722–1808) (line 123), one-time clergyman, wrote a successful tragedy, *Douglas* (1756), and was patronized by, and intimate with, Bute. John Ogilvie (1733–1813) (lines 126–7) published a long allegorical poem, 'Providence', in 1764. John Armstrong (1709–79) (lines 143–62) was the author of *Day* (1761), which had prompted Churchill's own *Night* (1761); he had also published a poem, 'Of Benevolence', in 1751; Churchill's animus against him relates to a breach between Armstrong and Wilkes in 1763, over Wilkes's abuse of the Scots in the *North Briton*.

There are some classical references. A 'siren' (line 41) was a bird-woman who would lure sailors onto the rocks; 'Pegasus' (line 89), a winged horse, often symbolizes supernatural power; the 'sisters of the hill' (line 91) is a humorous reference to the nine Muses on Mount Parnassus.

Some eighteenth-century usages may be obscure; 'phlegm' (line 65), deriving from medieval theories of the humours, signified a calm or apathetic temperament; 'Billingsgate' (line 82), London's fish market, was the home of proverbially foul-mouthed porters and vendors; 'dishabille' (line 92), from the French, *déshabillé*, meaning 'undressed', denotes informal or careless dress.

WILLIAM COWPER

To C.P., Ill with the Rheumatism

Probably written March 1752, in a letter to Chase Price, Cowper's friend since school at Westminster, and possibly a member of the Nonsense Club. Text derives from Price's Commonplace Book.

The central conceit of the poem presents poetry as curative, if written by the likes of Pope, Swift, or Samuel Butler (1613–80, author of 'Hudibras', a satirical poem, 1662–80); or at least soporific, if written by the likes of Sir Richard Blackmore (1654–1729, physician and inept poet), or indeed by Cowper himself. Richard Mead (1673–1754) in line 16 was a famous physician, one of whose patients was Pope; Sir Samuel Garth (1661–1719), in line 23, also a physician and friend of Pope's, wrote the satirical poem 'The Dispensary' (1699).

The poem, in keeping with the mock-heroic tone here, has a framework of classical allusion. The poet invokes the bewitching musical powers of Orpheus's lyre (line 1), and seeks to emulate Phoebus, or Apollo (lines 7–14), the god of healing as well as music. He alludes also (line 41) to Parnassus, the seat of the nine Muses in ancient Greece, and to Lethe (line 42), the river of forgetfulness in the underworld.

'Probatum est' (line 20) means 'it has been proved', and was a phrase used by eighteenth-century physicians in writing prescriptions. The 'torpedo' (line 32) is an electric ray.

'This Evening, Delia, You and I'

Written summer 1752. No manuscript copy survives; the text for this poem and the next is derived from Croft, *Poems, the Early Productions of William Cowper* (1825).

'Delia' was the poetical name which Cowper gave to his cousin Theadora (?1734–1824), with whom he was in love (they were never to marry). This is perhaps the earliest of the many poems he addressed to her between 1752 and 1755.

'Hope, Like the Short-lived Ray that Gleams Awhile'

Probably written summer 1755, after Cowper and Theadora had been finally forbidden to meet by her father, who took a dim view of Cowper's prospects.

'Doomed, as I am, in Solitude to Waste'

Written after (how long after is not known) 21 September 1757, on which date Cowper's close friend from schooldays, Sir William Russell, was drowned while swimming in the Thames. No manuscript copy survives; text from Hayley, *The Life, and Posthumous Writings, of William Cowper, Esqr.* (1803 first printing). The poem is probably addressed to Cowper's cousin Harriot (1733–1807), who later became Lady Hesketh (she married Thomas Hesketh, 1727–78, around 1754, and he was made a baronet in 1761).

Olney Hymns

Cowper made the acquaintance of John Newton (1725–1807), an ex-slave-trader turned Evangelical leader, in the summer of 1767. Cowper and Mrs Unwin, who was recently widowed, then moved to Newton's town of Olney, Buckinghamshire, in September 1767, and threw themselves into the Evangelical lifestyle. Cowper had been composing hymns (and little else) since his conversion in the summer of 1764; Newton encouraged him to compose more, and Newton's and Cowper's joint collection, entitled *Olney Hymns, in Three Books*, was published in 1779, from which edition the texts here are taken. Baird and Ryskamp observe that Newton, who oversaw publication, seems to have copied Cowper's hymns faithfully for private circulation, but made some revisions for publication; relevant variants are therefore noted below. Some of the hymns (e.g. number 35, printed here) appeared before 1779, in *Twenty Six Letters on Religious Subjects*, by 'Omicron' (Newton), 1774.

Light Shining out of Darkness

Written late 1772. The title alludes to *2 Peter* 1:19 ('a light that shineth in a dark place'), and *John* 1:5 ('And the light shineth in darkness'). See note on *Olney Hymns* above.

Line 20 exists differently in a transcript by Newton dated 18 February 1773: 'But *wait*, to *smell the flower*' (preserved in the Maitland–Madan Commonplace Book in the Bodleian Library; Newton sent the copy to Mrs Madan, the wife of Cowper's cousin Martin Madan).

Temptation

Date of composition unknown. Lines 1–8 allude to Christ's calming of the storm on Galilee, *Mark* 4:37–9. See note on *Olney Hymns* above.

Retirement

Written 1764 or 1765, soon after Cowper's conversion. See note on *Olney Hymns* above.

Some variants occur in a transcript by Newton in the Maitland–Madan Commonplace Book: line 18 has 'fount' for 'source'; line 19 has 'endearing' for 'harmonious'; and line 20 has 'I am thine!' for 'thou art mine!'.

'Hatred and Vengeance, My Eternal Portion'

Probably written 1774, during Cowper's second breakdown, when he became convinced of his own damnation. First published in Cox, *Memoirs of the Most Remarkable and Interesting Parts of the Life of William Cowper* (1816), from where the text here derives. Some variants exist in an undated transcript in Warwick Record Office, in the hand of George Courtenay, Cowper's landlord at Weston: line 6 has 'slew' for 'sold'; line 15 has 'Fall'n, and' for 'I'm called,'; and line 19 has 'filthy' for 'fleshly'.

There is a network of biblical allusions. For Judas's betrayal of Christ, see *Matthew* 26:14–16. For Abiram (lines 16–20), see *Numbers*, 16:30–3; he was one of the Israelite rebels whom God punished at Moses's request by having them swallowed alive into the earth. Line 19, 'fed with judgments', echoes *Ezekiel* 34:16, 'I will destroy the fat and the strong; I will feed them with judgment'.

The Bee and the Pineapple

Probably written between April and September 1779. Text derives from Cowper's record book, in his own hand, of poems 1779–81, in the Huntington Library, California.

To Mr. Newton on His Return from Ramsgate

Written 12–13 October 1780 and sent as part of a letter from Cowper to Newton, in response to one from Newton describing his visit to Ramsgate and including some verses on that 'storm-vex'd sea, the World'. Text derives from Cowper's record book of poems 1779–81.

For line 13, 'sea of troubles', see *Hamlet*, III. i. 60.

Verses, Supposed to be Written by Alexander Selkirk

Probably written before 1780. Published in the 1782 *Poems*, from where the text here is taken.

Alexander Selkirk (1676–1721) was marooned on the South American island of Juan Fernandez in October 1704 and rescued by Captain Woodes Rogers in February 1709. Rogers's *A Cruising Voyage round the World* (1712) related the story, which also inspired Defoe's *Robinson Crusoe* (1719).

Wordsworth discusses the 'poetic diction' of the fourth and fifth stanzas in his enlarged 1802 'Preface' to *Lyrical Ballads*, attacking lines 29–32 as artificial, but praising lines 33–40.

Lines 1–4 allude to *Genesis* 1:26–8, and Adam's dominion over the creation; lines 17–18 seem to refer to the gift of Eve. The poem's diction is frequently biblical; specifically, lines 25–8 echo *Psalms* 12:6, 19:9–10.

The Modern Patriot

The text used here was published in the 1782 *Poems*. Probably written June 1780, after the Gordon Riots, in which case the poem would be satirizing Lord George Gordon, President of the Protestant Association whose anti-Catholic agitations sparked off the Riots. But the poem may have been written earlier (February 1780) as an attack on the parliamentary opposition, with whose proposals for parliamentary reform, especially Edmund Burke's 'Plan for the Better Security of the Independence of Parliament', Cowper soon afterwards became more sympathetic. The 'roaring boys' at line 5 are the rebels against British rule in the American War of Independence.

The Winter Nosegay

Written November 1780. Published in the 1782 *Poems*, with the text used here.

Arcadia (line 9) is the region of Greece romanticized as the home of pastoral idyll; Flora (line 10) is the Roman goddess of flowering plants and fertility.

Boadicea, an Ode

Perhaps written in winter 1780; certainly extant by January 1781. Published in the 1782 *Poems*, with the text used here.

Obviously inspired by Gray's 'The Bard', Cowper's poem, in tune with late eighteenth-century imperialist confidence, more optimistically envisages national glory, albeit long after the death of the poem's protagonist. Boadicea (d. AD 62), Queen of the Iceni tribe of eastern England, led a bloody but futile revolt against Roman rule in AD 59–60. Lines 21–4 perhaps convey Boadicea's attack on the effeminate musical interests of the emperor Nero; they may also refer to the eighteenth-century dominance of Italian singers in the London theatre.

The Poet, the Oyster, and Sensitive Plant

Date not known. First published in the 1782 *Poems*, with the text used here.
At line 49, 'grotto-work' means shell-encrusted rather than cave-like.

To the Rev. William Cawthorne Unwin

Published in the 1782 *Poems*, with the text used here. Probably written late March/April 1781; later, in early May, Cowper sent a copy in a letter to Unwin, soothing Unwin's hurt feelings at not having been informed of the projected 1782 *Poems* by insisting that these lines of tribute had already been sent to the publisher, Joseph Johnson.

The language in lines 13–18 is of horticultural inoculating and strengthening, and is accurate – as one might expect from Cowper, who was a keen gardener.

On the Loss of the Royal George

Written either September 1782 or, more probably, July 1782. Sent in an undated letter to Unwin. First printed by Hayley, 1803; text used here derives from Cowper's letter to Unwin (now in the British Library), thus retaining Cowper's original Alexandrine lines (required by the verses' musical setting) which early editors bisected.

The *Royal George* sank on 29 August 1782. Cowper may well have read of the disaster in *Gentleman's Magazine*, 52 (August, 1782), 405. Richard Kempenfelt (1718–82), an Englishman of Swedish descent, was a notable seaman, active in sea-battles against the French, and appointed Rear-Admiral of the Blue in 1780.

Epitaph on a Hare

Written 7 March 1783, in a letter to the Rev. William Bull. First printed *Gentleman's Magazine*, 54 (December, 1784), 935, with (apparently) editorial revisions; thus, the text here derives from Cowper's entry book of his poems 1781–93 (now in the Huntington Library, California), which closely follows the 1783 draft.

The *Gentleman's Magazine*, 54 (June, 1784), 412–14, had earlier printed Cowper's essay on his three hares, Puss, Tiney and Bess, a charming account of their habits, character and dietary requirements.

'Puss' (line 40) is glossed by Johnson's *Dictionary* (1756) not only as 'the fondling name of a cat', but also as 'the sportsman's term for a hare'; see Gay's *Fables* (1727), number 50, 'The Hare and many Friends', line 29. Johnson also notes that 'Jack' (line 8) is 'the male of animals'.

The Poplar-Field

Probably written in summer 1783. First printed in *Gentleman's Magazine*, 55 (January, 1785), 53; subsequently revised by Cowper, and copied, probably in 1791, into his entry book of poems 1781–93, from where the text here derives.

Cowper expands upon the poem's context in a letter to Lady Hesketh, 1 May 1786, where the scene is located in the parish of Lavendon, near Olney. The Ouse (line 4) is the river which runs through Olney.

To the Immortal Memory of the Halibut

Written in a letter to William Unwin, 25–6 April 1784, thanking him for the present of a fish (and a lobster). First printed by John Johnson in *Private Correspondence of William Cowper* (2 vols., 1824), but incomplete; text here is from Cowper's draft in the letter to Unwin, collated (following Baird and Ryskamp) with Johnson.

The Latinate names for countries (Batavia = the Netherlands, Caledonia = Scotland, Hibernia = Ireland, whose Giant's Causeway is referred to at line 18) are in keeping with the poem's mock-heroic tone.

from *Tirocinium: or, a Review of Schools*

Begun in autumn 1782; finished October/November 1784. Printed in *The Task*, 1785, with the text used here.

In the 1770s, Cowper had considered giving private tuition in his own home; in 1780, he and Unwin, himself a father who educated his two sons at home, corresponded about the respective advantages of domestic and public-school education. Cowper was apparently fired to complete the poem in 1784 after learning that Westminster School (which he and Churchill had attended in the 1740s) now kept a surgeon to treat the boys' venereal diseases (see *Letters*, ii. 302). In the 'Advertisement' which prefaced *The Task*, however, Cowper stresses that 'he would be very sorry to stand suspected of having aimed his censure at any particular school. His objections are such as naturally apply themselves to schools in general.'

'Tirocinium' is a Latin word meaning 'a soldier's first service', or 'pupilage'; cf. 'tiro' at line 220, passage (i), meaning a novice.

(i)

'Bacchanalian' (line 214), derives from Bacchus, the Greek and Roman god of wine and debauchery. Line 222 refers to the election, at Westminster School in particular, of certain boys as King's Scholars (Churchill was thus elected in 1745); the chief of these was Captain of his Election.

Line 230, 'hair-breadth scapes', echoes Othello's boasted exploits, *Othello*, I. iii. 136.

(ii)

'taw' (line 307) was a game of marbles, which involved crouching (or 'knuckling') down to roll them. The 'grounded hat' (line 308) is perhaps an improvised wicket for a form of cricket.

The Winter Evening (*Book IV of* The Task)

Written between September 1783 and October 1784; probably after December 1783. First printed in *The Task* 1785, the text used here. There are six books in all of Cowper's great discursive poem on national affairs and rural life:–

1. The Sofa – prompted by a challenge from Lady Austen to write a blank verse poem on the subject – which blossomed into successive books:
2. The Time-Piece
3. The Garden
4. The Winter Evening
5. The Winter Morning Walk
6. The Winter Walk at Noon.

Aspects of the final three books may well have been inspired by a severe frost on 19 December 1783, which lasted over two months, and especially heavy snow on 29 December 1783.

The beginning of Book IV, 'The Winter Evening', describes the arrival and reading of the daily letters and, more importantly, the newspapers (cf. Crabbe's poem, 'The Newspaper', 1785), both delivered by the post office in the eighteenth century. In 1783–4 Cowper subscribed to the *Morning Chronicle* and *London Advertiser*. The 'budget' (line 23), a word originally signifying a bag, is a collection of news items, or, indeed, a newspaper. The random arrangement of news, parliamentary reports, editorial comment, gossip, and advertisements (for beauty treatments and remedies, lines 79–83), characteristic of eighteenth-century newspapers, is well evoked in lines 55–87. Dr Gustavus Katterfelto (d. 1799), line 86, was a sensationalist quack in London; line 85 refers to the current interest in ballooning, following Montgolfier's successful flight in the summer of 1783, and, more obscurely, contemporary experiments with diving bells. Lines 25–35 evoke specific political issues: the loss of America (lines 25–7), which Cowper here attributes to the feeble spirit of the English generals; the controversial conduct of the East India Company, and Anglo-French hostilities in India (lines 28–30), which had only recently ceased; and debates in the House of Commons (fully reported in the newspapers, especially the *Morning Chronicle*) on Fox's proposed India Bills in the winter of 1783–4 (lines 30–3, 46–9). The *Morning Chronicle* also featured theatre reviews, see lines 43–5. The 'patriots' referred to in lines 48–9 are those in opposition to the government, who prided themselves on the defence of 'liberty'; they are contrasted with the 'placemen', appointees of the crown. Lord Shelburne (lines 57–63), here representing 'ambition', was ousted by Fox and North in February 1783; they in turn (line 63) were replaced by Pitt in December 1783. In lines 39–40, Cowper's famous celebration of tea, he in fact echoes George Berkeley's *Siris* (1744), which praises the ability of tar-water to 'cheer but not inebriate'.

At line 88, Cowper shifts his focus to the rural retreat from the urban 'Babel' (see *Genesis* 11:9 for the city of many languages). The voyages he enjoys from his armchair in lines 107–19 evince Cowper's interest in travel writing, the most consistently popular genre of the eighteenth century (cf. 'Verses Supposed to be Written by Alexander Selkirk' and 'The Castaway'). The reference to winter as the 'inverted year' at line 120 derives from Horace, *Satires*, I. i. 36. Lines 150–66 evoke the evening pursuits (with a distinctly feminine cast) of the Cowper household, comprising Mary Unwin and, at this stage, Lady Austen, who was musical. Lines 168–73 liken their frugal catering to the asceticism of the Roman republic; 'a radish and an egg' refers specifically to a meal served to Jupiter and Mercury by Baucis and Philemon in Ovid, *Metamorphoses*, VIII. 666–7. The 'Sabine bard' at line 190 is Horace, whose lifestyle, once he had retired to his farm in the Sabine hills, has many affinities with Cowper's.

At line 194, Cowper reverts, for contrast, to the urban sophistication he has rejected. The 'tragic fur' at line 195 is ermine, a badge of high rank, and worn by tragic actors in the theatre to signify the dignity of their character; Cowper's concern for animal welfare may also be relevant here. The attack on cards (lines 207–31), traditionally a winter, specifically Christmas, pursuit, seems partly to echo Pope's *Rape of the Lock*, III. 25–100. A billiard 'mast', line 221 (altered in some later editions to 'mace') is a cue. A 'back-string' (line 227) is a child's pinafore.

The invocation to Evening (lines 242–60) is Miltonic, echoing in particular 'Il Penseroso', 31–8, and *Paradise Lost*, IV. 598–609. Lines 254–8 evoke a moon low in the sky (in evening's 'purple zone') and therefore particularly rounded. For Goliath (whom Milton, 'Samson Agonistes', 1249, also spells Goliah), see *1 Samuel* 17:4–7.

Lines 267–332, which reject Locke's model of the human mind in favour of a more imaginative, creative mode (a 'soul that does not always think', line 285), exerted an influence on later Romantic poets, especially Coleridge (see 'Frost at Midnight', which echoes Cowper's reference to 'sooty films', traditional harbingers of a visit). 'mercurial' at line 282 means lively or active. Lines 326–32 echo Thomson's *Winter*, 229–40; 'lapse' (line 327) means a soft falling, and 'assimilate' (line 329) means to make similar.

Lines 333–73 are unlikely to endear Cowper to modern readers; they describe the happy insensibility of the lower classes to aspects of the weather which fell more refined individuals. The 'unhealthful' East wind is proverbial; Pope, in *The Rape of the Lock*, IV, 424, associates it with spleen (an upper-class malady).

Cowper described lines 374–424 as 'a family-piece taken from the life' (letter to Robert Smith, 31 December 1784). The reference to the 'taper soon extinguished' (line 391) evinces Cowper's disapproval of Pitt's unjust tax on candles, which hit the poor in particular; a 'skillet' (line 402) is a cooking pot. Lines 410–19 refer to the problematic system by which the poor had to apply for relief from unpopular local overseers. Lines 427–9 pay tribute to Robert Smith (1752–1828, banker and MP for Nottingham), who sent £20 in January, and again in February 1784, for the anonymous relief of Olney's poor.

Lines 429–512 present an anatomy of drunkenness ('ebriety', line 460) and its evil effects on society. A 'pale' (line 436) is a wooden fence; 'plashed' (line 437) means split and plaited, probably with sapling stems; the detail of 'an ass's burthen' (line 441) conveys that the load is large, more than a man alone would usually carry. Alehouses, licensed by Justices of the Peace (line 471), which Cowper here presents as filled with tobacco smoke ('Indian fume', line 473) and intoxicated artisans ('Lethean' at line 475 derives from Lethe, the river of forgetfulness in the classical underworld), in fact provided the government with much-needed revenue, especially in times of war (lines 509–12), through the imposition of duties. Midas (line 507), King of Phrygia, turned everything he touched to gold.

Lines 513–612 lament the luxury and immorality of modern life, and the loss, even in the country, of the pastoral innocence embodied in the *Eclogues* of Virgil (Maro, line 515) and in *The Countess of Pembroke's Arcadia* (1590) by Sir Philip Sidney. The reference to Diana (line 517) is specifically to her chastity – not, apparently, a characteristic of modern nymphs. The Latinate 'tramontane' at line 533 means, literally, beyond the mountains (specifically, Alps); effectively, it means 'beyond our ability to imagine' or, perhaps, 'outlandish'. Cowper laments the corruption of rustic innocence by fashionable absurdities: 'lappets' (line 540) are decorative streamers. Fashion becomes a symbol of national corruption or 'luxury', a frequent bugbear of eighteenth-century moralists; see John Sekora, *Luxury: The Concept in Western Thought from Eden to Smollett* (Baltimore, 1977). The dallying of the aristocracy in London, to the neglect of their country seats (lines 587–92), was likewise a frequent cause for complaint. Landowners, or Justices of the Peace ('Authority' in line 593), might delegate their duties to idle and corruptible country parsons (lines 595–612), willing to be bribed (here, by poachers, lines 611–12) for a favourable hearing or 'audit' (line 610).

Lines 613–58 attack the militia, instituted in 1757 and not dismantled until 1783: men aged between eighteen and fifty were chosen by ballot (line 627) to serve for three years in the local regiment, officered by the local gentry. In wartime – though not in peace – this service would entail permanent training and action away from home. By 1783, the local militias were disbanding, filling the countryside with disaffected and jobless ex-soldiers. The 'meal and larded locks' at line 642 refers to the greasing and flouring of soldiers' ponytails; a 'clown' at line 623 is simply a peasant or rustic.

Lines 659–90 draw a contrast between natural social bonds, and those constructed by the state and by commercial interests, such as 'chartered boroughs' (line 671), independent bodies of local authority, granted by royal charter, and especially liable to corruption. The 'merchants' at line 676 are the East India Company, whose charter gave them extraordinary power over the Indians, much criticized by liberal politicians. The 'field of glory', here ironic (line 684), refers to military service, another corrupt institution (lines 684–90).

At this point, Cowper returns, for the remainder of 'The Winter Evening', to 'the country', dwelling not on its shortcomings but on the power of Nature to heal and purify the mind. Pastoral poetry is again invoked, this time more optimistically, as a true reflection of life and especially Nature; 'Tityrus' (line 707) is from Virgil's *Eclogues*, lines 710–17 pay tribute to Milton's *Paradise Lost*, and lines 718–30 to Abraham Cowley (1618–67), a poet admired by Pope but whose 'ingenious' and learned wit ('the cobwebs of the schools') became increasingly uncongenial to later eighteenth-century tastes. He retired to Chertsey in Surrey in 1665. Lines 748–79 evoke the changing face of suburban London, which was sprawling outwards from its polluted centre ('Like a swarth Indian', line 749).

Lines 780–801, somewhat in the manner of Pope's *Essay on Man*, evoke an ordered universe in which every individual is placed in his appropriate setting. The 'deliverer of an injured land' (line 793) is probably Fox, who campaigned on behalf of the Indians oppressed by the East India Company. Cowper places himself within 'the low vale of life' (line 799), alluding beautifully to Gray's 'Elegy', line 75, 'the cool sequestered vale of life'.

Verses Subjoined to the Bill of Mortality for the Town of Northampton, 1787

Written 19–27 November 1787. First printed in the Bill of Mortality for Northampton, December 1787. Cowper subsequently transcribed the poem several times in letters, from the latest of which, to Newton,

19 February 1788, the text here derives. The motto is from Horace, *Odes*
I. iv. 13–14.

In November 1787, Cowper was asked by the parish clerk of All Saints'
Church in Northampton to supply verses to the parish's Bill of Mortality
that year. Cowper contributed such verses for the next six years (except
1791). The 1787 poem rhetorically purports (see lines 29–36) to be written
by this clerk, John Cox; his church duties included making the responses
('Amen', line 36) during services. The river Nene (line 2) runs through
Northampton. There is an echo of *Twelfth Night*, II. iv. 112–13 ('conceal-
ment like a worm i' th' bud') at line 23, and biblical echoes at lines 17–20
(*Psalms* 37:35–6), and line 21 (*Habakkuk* 2:2).

Pity for Poor Africans

One of four poems Cowper wrote against the slave trade. Written before
9 August 1788; probably early July 1788. No manuscript survives. First
printed in *Northampton Mercury*, 9 August 1788, from where the text here
derives. The motto is from Ovid, *Metamorphoses*, VIII. 20–1.

France, the Netherlands and Denmark (line 9) all had West Indian
colonies. This argument (lines 9–12) was frequently advanced in defence
of the slave trade. To 'go snacks' (line 16) is to divide the profits.

On the Receipt of my Mother's Picture out of Norfolk

Written between 27 February, when Cowper wrote to Mrs Bodham to
thank her for the picture, and 8 March 1790, when he writes to Lady
Hesketh that the poem is completed. In January 1790, a young cousin, John
Johnson, called on Cowper; the visit re-established links with the Norfolk
branch of the family. Johnson became an eager transcriber of Cowper's
poems, and another Norfolk cousin, Mrs Ann Bodham, sent to Cowper
the miniature of his mother, Anne Donne Cowper (1703–37), by a German
painter D. Heins, which prompted the poem. Text here is from Cowper's
entry book of poems 1781–93, in John Johnson's hand. A version published
in a pamphlet by Joseph Johnson, Cowper's publisher, in 1798 (and later
included in a two-volume *Poems* in the same year) seems to date from an
earlier stage of composition.

Cowper's mother died in 1737, two days before his sixth birthday, while
the family inhabited Berkhamsted Rectory (the 'Pastoral house' of line 53).
Cowper's father, the Revd John Cowper, died (line 99) in 1756. There is
little that is obscure in this poem. 'Elysian' in line 19 means blessed, derived
from the Greek Elysium, or paradise; 'humour' in line 67 means whim, or
change of mood; lines 74–7 describe the young Cowper making a tracing,
with a pin, of the embroidered pattern on his mother's dress.

Line 72, 'frail memorial', echoes Gray's 'Elegy', line 78; and the imagery of voyage and shipwreck in the poem's closing passage (line 88 onwards) is increasingly characteristic of Cowper in his later years; cf. a letter to Newton, 13 January 1787, in which he describes his life as 'the most turbulent voyage that ever Christian mariner made'. Newey, *Cowper's Poetry*, 245–70, has a fine discussion of the poem's place within the eighteenth-century elegiac tradition, and of its status as an early 'Romantic' lyric.

Yardley Oak

Probably written summer 1791. William Hayley discovered the manuscript and printed it in 1803. The manuscript remains in the Cowper and Newton Museum in Olney and is the source for the text here.

British and classical myth, and the Bible, figure in the poem. Druids (lines 10–11) were associated with the oak tree ('*drus*' in Greek); Cowper here (lines 11–14) alludes to the spiritual darkness of the druids, who lived before the crucifixion ('act/Of amnesty', lines 12–13; a 'meed' is a reward). The 'fabled twins' at line 35 are Castor and Pollux, allegedly born from one egg (paralleling the twin lobes within an acorn), who were turned into stars (Gemini) after their death. 'Dodona' (line 41) is the ancient Greek oracle, voiced by oak trees. Lines 146–8 describe Cowper measuring the years of a lifespan on the oak's trunk; he refers (lines 149–54) to *Genesis* 47:9, where Jacob (130 years old) announces that 'few and evil have the days of my life been'; and *Genesis* 5, which describes the long life of the patriarchs before Noah.

The 'glebe' at line 26 is a Latinate term for the soil; similarly, 'champain' at line 53 is a field or meadow. A 'searce' (line 30) is a sieve or strainer. Lines 64–6 are especially Miltonic in their word order and consciously lofty tone, characteristic of the poem's mock-sublimity. William Ruddick, in 'Liberty Trees and Loyal Oaks', in Alison Yarrington and Kelvin Everest, eds., *Reflections of Revolution: Images of Romanticism* (London and New York, 1993), pp. 59–67, presents an important political reading of the poem. Ruddick observes how Cowper subtly probes Burke's optimistically organicist theories of society; in 'Yardley Oak', decay is as inevitable as growth. See also Newey, *Cowper's Poetry*, 42–4.

The poem's dangling conclusion is intriguing; it is probably incomplete, but may just be an early example of 'Romantic' fragmentation; cf. Keats's 'Hyperion', and Coleridge's 'Kubla Khan'.

To the Nightingale

Perhaps written in spring 1792; in a letter to John Johnson, 11 March 1792, Cowper refers to the good omen of having 'heard a Nightingale on New-year's day'. By March 1792, Mrs Unwin was recovering from a serious stroke of December 1791, and her recovery may be implied in the 'happier days at hand' of line 16. Text here derives from Cowper's entry book of poems 1781–93, in John Johnson's hand.

In Greek mythology, Philomela (line 9) was raped by her brother-in-law, Tereus, who then cut out her tongue to silence her; she was turned into a nightingale.

To Mary

Written 1792 or 1793, twenty years after Cowper's serious depression of January 1773 (alluded to in lines 1–2). Text is derived from Cowper's manuscript in the Cowper and Newton Museum, Olney. Hayley printed it in 1803, omitting lines 37–40, perhaps because they insinuate romantic feelings for Mrs Unwin.

The Castaway

Written 19–25 March 1799. Text derives from the 'Norfolk Manuscripts' of poems 1799–1800; there is a facsimile in *Princeton University Library Chronicle*, 26 (1962–3), 23–4. First published by Hayley in 1803.

The last poem Cowper wrote in English, 'The Castaway' was inspired by an account of a man overboard which Cowper read in Richard Walter's *A Voyage round the World by George Anson* (1748), a more polished version of Anson's own ship's log, referred to at lines 49–52. Anson is the brave 'Chief' at lines 7–8. 'Albion' at lines 7 and 9 is England.

Cowper employs the story as a grim metaphor for his own spiritual state; 'castaway' in the eighteenth-century generally had the theological sense of 'reprobate', as in *1 Corinthians* 9:27; Cowper's sense of personal damnation pervades the poem, which contains echoes of his previous works, such as 'Light Shining out of Darkness' and 'Temptation' from *Olney Hymns*. The figure of Christ calming the waters (*Matthew* 8:26, *Mark* 4:37–9; cf. 'Temptation', lines 5–8) is invoked only to be pronounced absent (lines 61–2).

INDEX OF TITLES

INDEX OF FIRST LINES

READ MORE IN PENGUIN

In every corner of the world, on every subject under the sun, Penguin represents quality and variety – the very best in publishing today.

For complete information about books available from Penguin – including Puffins, Penguin Classics and Arkana – and how to order them, write to us at the appropriate address below. Please note that for copyright reasons the selection of books varies from country to country.

In the United Kingdom: Please write to *Dept. EP, Penguin Books Ltd, Bath Road, Harmondsworth, West Drayton, Middlesex UB7 0DA*

In the United States: Please write to *Consumer Sales, Penguin USA, P.O. Box 999, Dept. 17109, Bergenfield, New Jersey 07621-0120.* VISA and MasterCard holders call 1-800-253-6476 to order Penguin titles

In Canada: Please write to *Penguin Books Canada Ltd, 10 Alcorn Avenue, Suite 300, Toronto, Ontario M4V 3B2*

In Australia: Please write to *Penguin Books Australia Ltd, P.O. Box 257, Ringwood, Victoria 3134*

In New Zealand: Please write to *Penguin Books (NZ) Ltd, Private Bag 102902, North Shore Mail Centre, Auckland 10*

In India: Please write to *Penguin Books India Pvt Ltd, 706 Eros Apartments, 56 Nehru Place, New Delhi 110 019*

In the Netherlands: Please write to *Penguin Books Netherlands bv, Postbus 3507, NL-1001 AH Amsterdam*

In Germany: Please write to *Penguin Books Deutschland GmbH, Metzlerstrasse 26, 60594 Frankfurt am Main*

In Spain: Please write to *Penguin Books S. A., Bravo Murillo 19, 1° B, 28015 Madrid*

In Italy: Please write to *Penguin Italia s.r.l., Via Felice Casati 20, I–20124 Milano*

In France: Please write to *Penguin France S. A., 17 rue Lejeune, F–31000 Toulouse*

In Japan: Please write to *Penguin Books Japan, Ishikiribashi Building, 2–5–4, Suido, Bunkyo-ku, Tokyo 112*

In South Africa: Please write to *Longman Penguin Southern Africa (Pty) Ltd, Private Bag X08, Bertsham 2013*

READ MORE IN PENGUIN

A CHOICE OF CLASSICS

Armadale Wilkie Collins

Victorian critics were horrified by Lydia Gwilt, the bigamist, husband-poisoner and laudanum addict whose intrigues spur the plot of this most sensational of melodramas.

Aurora Leigh and Other Poems Elizabeth Barrett Browning

Aurora Leigh (1856), Elizabeth Barrett Browning's epic novel in blank verse, tells the story of the making of a woman poet, exploring 'the woman question', art and its relation to politics and social oppression.

Personal Narrative of a Journey to the Equinoctial Regions of the New Continent Alexander von Humboldt

Alexander von Humboldt became a wholly new kind of nineteenth-century hero – the scientist–explorer – and in *Personal Narrative* he invented a new literary genre: the travelogue.

The Pañćatantra Visnu Sarma

The Pañćatantra is one of the earliest books of fables and its influence can be seen in the *Arabian Nights*, the *Decameron*, the *Canterbury Tales* and most notably in the *Fables* of La Fontaine.

A Laodicean Thomas Hardy

The Laodicean of Hardy's title is Paula Power, a thoroughly modern young woman who, despite her wealth and independence, cannot make up her mind.

Brand Henrik Ibsen

The unsparing vision of a priest driven by faith to risk and witness the deaths of his wife and child gives *Brand* its icy ferocity. It was Ibsen's first masterpiece, a poetic drama composed in 1865 and published to tremendous critical and popular acclaim.

READ MORE IN PENGUIN

A CHOICE OF CLASSICS

Francis Bacon	**The Essays**
Aphra Behn	**Love-Letters between a Nobleman and His Sister**
	Oroonoko, The Rover and Other Works
George Berkeley	**Principles of Human Knowledge/Three Dialogues between Hylas and Philonous**
James Boswell	**The Life of Samuel Johnson**
Sir Thomas Browne	**The Major Works**
John Bunyan	**The Pilgrim's Progress**
Edmund Burke	**Reflections on the Revolution in France**
Frances Burney	**Evelina**
Margaret Cavendish	**The Blazing World and Other Writings**
William Cobbett	**Rural Rides**
William Congreve	**Comedies**
Thomas de Quincey	**Confessions of an English Opium Eater**
	Recollections of the Lakes and the Lake Poets
Daniel Defoe	**A Journal of the Plague Year**
	Moll Flanders
	Robinson Crusoe
	Roxana
	A Tour Through the Whole Island of Great Britain
Henry Fielding	**Amelia**
	Jonathan Wild
	Joseph Andrews
	The Journal of a Voyage to Lisbon
	Tom Jones
John Gay	**The Beggar's Opera**
Oliver Goldsmith	**The Vicar of Wakefield**
Lady Gregory	**Selected Writings**

READ MORE IN PENGUIN

A CHOICE OF CLASSICS